This book is like Dave Barry meets Tom Peters at Danielle Steel's place.

—James McNamara, North Carolina

I took the book home, my husband devoured it — I'm shocked, he never reads!

— C. Huml, Ft. Lauderdale

A business lesson, without the pain, a love lesson with the pain— who knew?

— Dee Gykes, New Orleans

The writing equivalent of shooting the curl.

— John Felton, San Jose, California

Sara

We hope you will enjoy the Adventure

ADVENTURE CAPITAL

JOHN RUSHING

A Dandelion Books Publication
Tempe, Arizona

A Dandelion Books Publication
Dandelion Enterprises
Tempe, Arizona

www:dandelionbooks.com

Library of Congress Cataloging-in-Publication Data

Rushing, John
Adventure Capital

Library of Congress Catalog Card Number 00-108638
ISBN 1-893302-08-3

Cover and interior design by Irin Smith, www.mediamagica.com; printed by Lightning Source, Inc.

This book is dedicated to Mary Felton Rushing who gave me life and who provided an example of diligence and persistence, tempered with humor and a caring nature.

This book would not have been possible without the support and encouragement of my wife Sherrie, who lived not just through the writing process but who endured the actual adventures upon which the novel is based. Nor could the book have seen the light of day without the dedicated help of Carol Adler, my editor and friend, who early on saw potential in what started as a compressed outpouring of thought and emotion.

CHAPTER ONE
THE SENATOR

"A bribe," he thought. "The bitch wants a bribe."

Limpid brown eyes scanned Mark, seeking any reaction, any change in expression. There was none. He was young and damned good looking, with a rugged body that LL Bean would use to peddle anything from Rugby shirts to running shorts. Jade green eyes, clear lightly freckled skin that softened his chiseled features. Hair like burnt umber, still burning. Smart? She wondered.

"Senator —"

"Please, Mr. Hansen — Mark," she interrupted as she came out from behind her desk, "call me Connie. My friends do." She sat down in the chair opposite him and allowed her skirt to ride up above her knee.

"Senator . . . Connie . . . I'm not sure I understand just what you're suggesting." He knew damn well. He just wanted her to say it.

"Look around, Mark," her hand swept the room, "tell me what you see."

"Marble, wood, paintings, all expensive — very Senatorial."

That was an understatement. Mark estimated that the desk alone cost more than his car. The paintings were almost certainly originals and included what was probably an early Picasso. Not that he cared.

"And —"

"I don't know. Leather, furniture . . ." He had little patience with the game playing, but had no choice if he wanted her help. And . . . you."

She ran a hand over her knee and let it slide down the side of her leg. Mark tried not to look at her legs, tried not to fall into those gorgeous brown eyes.

She lowered her voice. "Mark, look at it this way. I am a U. S. Senator and this is my office. You are a citizen who's looking for some help getting your product – your invention, on the market. You need to cut through some red tape so you can – what? Save someone lost at sea? Get rich and retire — whatever. She paused, again scanning for a response.

Mark nodded and a faint trace of a grin briefly flashed across his face. Connie continued, "Assume for now my husband is not the Secretary of Transportation and that you didn't come to me because he controls the people you need to see."

"I'm not sure what you're driving at," he said haltingly, "but my associates —"

"are wonderful people whom I have not had the pleasure of meeting," she interrupted pointedly.

"All that aside . . . We, my associates and I, feel strongly about your candidacy. We wonder how you would feel if we were to form a PAC and provide some support for your re-election." He paused, scanning her carefully. Nothing. Not a twitch, not one nostril move; nothing.

"Well, Mark that is very thoughtful, but you know some people might misunderstand such support." What would her husband think of him, she wondered. The senator's smile broadened.

Mark caught himself bathing in her smile. It was warm. Hell it was devastating. No wonder she was so effective. She could melt titanium with that smile. But not him.

"I hadn't thought of it like that." A white lie. He didn't think this up, his associates did. "But maybe my people could talk with your people and come up with a suitable way for handling such matters so we could avoid any, uh—possible *misunderstandings.*"

"Maybe so. So . . . why don't you suggest that to your associates?" Connie stood up, casually smoothing her skirt. Even in a blue business suit, white blouse and practical coiffure, she was a show stopper. Tall, maybe five ten in flats, fit, yet round. Not Rubinesque, but round, very round. She moved toward his chair.

Mark rose, assuming he was being dismissed. He was only half right.

"Mark, I have a vote on the Senate floor, but I would like to continue our conversation. My secretary will arrange it." She extended her hand, "We are always happy to serve our constituents."

He was left standing awkwardly with his "thank you" trailing her out the door.

Alfred, the senator's secretary was waiting for him, pencil poised over the appointment book. "Senator Johnson will be available Friday at 11:30. Will that be satisfactory?" He peered at Mark over his antique spectacles.

"Lunch would be good," Mark started.

"No sir." Alfred cleared his throat, making no effort to hide his amusement. "Sir, this would be PM. 11:30 PM, at the Gateway Hotel, suite 516."

"Oh, uh . . . that's fine too," Mark stammered. "Thanks."

"Here is an appointment card, with the time and the address. Attire will be casual, sir."

Mark almost asked what "casual" meant, but decided he could figure that out well enough. Figuring out how Alfred was able to set the appointment so quickly was another matter, although maybe that wasn't so difficult after all.

Friday came quickly. He managed to keep busy, doing the obligatory ride on the underground, the grand tour. The monuments. The memorials, a few good-byes at the Viet Nam wall, souvenir shopping . . . It was hot and the city was loaded with tourists. Hell, why should he complain? He was one, too, wasn't he? Well, not exactly. The only reason he'd made the trip, especially at this time of the year, was because he had to. *All the way*, he told himself resolutely, hailing a cab and glancing at his watch. Six more hours before he was due.

Mark wondered what he should or should not say to the Senator. She obviously knew enough about his invention to understand that her husband could make or break Mark's business. But how much did she know about his partners and the deal he was proposing; anyway, would it matter?

A light drizzle was cooling the air as Mark stepped out of the cab in front of the Gateway. He looked around before entering. The Gateway had become a part of public consciousness when the conspiracy had unraveled there. Today, it was just one more fancy DC hotel where pols hung their hats and wannabes came and went.

The street, usually populated by panhandlers and vagrants, was silent. That was a relief. At least the rain was good for something. The panhandlers were way past aggressive. Many were openly threatening like the punks in Miami that offered to wash you car windows, or break them.

Mark pushed past the rotating glass doors and into the lobby, glanced at the card and proceeded to the fifth floor.

The door snapped open as if gripped by a powerful spring. "Mark, come on in, Connie will be with us in a few minutes." The muscular man motioned toward the interior. "I'm Bill, Connie's husband. She's been delayed but is on the way and asked me to hold the fort. May I offer you something to drink while we wait?"

Mark looked past him into the room. It was large, sparsely yet elegantly furnished. It looked unused, uninhabited; strangely so. It seemed to emphasize the strange informality with which he was treated. One doesn't expect the Secretary of Transportation to jump to a first name basis with a total stranger.

"Coke, water, anything's fine," Mark replied as they walked into the room. Bill was wearing a blue pin-striped suit and his gray hair peppered with brown was cut short military fashion. Like Connie he appeared fit, but definitely was not round. More like a halfback, and nearly as tall as Mark.

"Pepsi okay?" He passed the can to Mark, then eased into a chair, motioning to another chair for his guest.

Mark noticed Bill favored one leg as he sat. He understood that Bill had been wounded in battle. He also understood that Bill did not appreciate it very much when people made a point of noticing it.

Bill continued, "Connie tells me you're having a little problem with some of my people."

"Well, yes." Mark gulped a deep breath and dived in. "I am not sure how much of the background you know, but —"

"Let me save you a long dog and pony show. You need help. The wheels of bureaucracy turn slowly, if at all. You need to speed up the process and more importantly you need a favorable outcome. You cannot even get in the door. That about it?"

"Yes, but —"

"Do you have any idea of how many people are in exactly the same position as you and your partners?" He stared reflectively out over the city, then snapped his gaze back to Mark. "Never mind, it was a rhetorical question," he paused reflecting, "Anyway, Connie has taken a liking to you, probably something to do with her . . . well, anyway . . ."

This time the pause was much longer, leaving Mark wondering if he would continue. He wondered what Bill had omitted.

Bill, now looking more than his sixty years continued. "This is a very delicate thing. I've looked at your locator invention, at your particular situation, and frankly it looks questionable. You probably do not know that the government tried a similar idea and never could get the damn thing to work.

If I stick my neck out and suggest — I can't order, an okay — and if things go wrong . . ."

Mark leaned forward. "Oh, but they won't — not with this device! The entire system has been tested. It's bulletproof. And furthermore —"

"No offense, but I've heard that before," the Secretary

interrupted. "Mark, this is an act of faith on my part. I'm the one who will get the bad press, and worse than that, I'm the one who will be pegged as a meddling jerkoff by the troops." He paused again, but this time a faint smile crept across his lips. "Of course, it wouldn't be the first time, in either case."

"Does that mean that you —"

"It means I'll seriously consider it. But there's another matter that's even pricklier." The smile vanished. "If you and your people choose to support Connie in her re-election bid and I arrange to help you, some cynical people might misunderstand my motive, your motive — and more importantly my wife's motives." He stopped to make sure Mark fully got the message. "I would take it very unkindly if there were anything bad that happened to Connie as a result of this."

Mark had heard rumors about Bill's extra-governmental connections. He knew what he was being told. The consequences of a screw-up would be ugly, probably terminally ugly.

"Sir, I understand your concern, both for the Senator and yourself, as well as for me and my people. I can only vouch for myself. You'll have to make your own decisions about everyone else."

Bill eased back in his chair. He understood why Connie liked the kid. Still, he wondered just how much had to do with the PAC, the situation, and . . . and the kid was young . . . and . . . he *did* see the resemblance . . .

His musing was interrupted by a familiar rapping at the door.

Connie slipped into the room and moved to Bill. She hugged him allowing her hand to slip around his back and gently rub while she kissed his cheeks. She whispered something in his ear and for an instant Mark felt as if he were an intruder in some special private moment.

Breaking the embrace, Connie smiled at Mark, motioning him back into his chair. She was wearing a simple gown with a floral print, and she looked ravishing as she perched on the bed and fluffed out the folds of her skirt, spreading them around her. Bill returned to his chair.

"So you gentlemen have had a chance to get acquainted while I was playing dodgem with the press?"

As Mark watched Bill he understood. He would do anything short of murder for her. Maybe even that. It was touching in some bizarre way. But everyone had an agenda, including himself, and his agenda was deeper, broader and more compelling than any other. Whatever happened to anyone else, it would just have to happen.

"Yes," Bill replied, "but I think all the guy talk is over for now and I have to check in with the troops. We have a little situation in the Caribbean." He rose, moved directly to the door and paused. "Mark, nice meeting you. Connie, see you later." He was gone.

Connie rose and headed toward the rear of the room. "Mark, I'm going to freshen up. Just make yourself comfortable. There is TV and stereo, I'll just be a minute."

Puzzled, Mark watched her open the door and exit. He heard water running as if a bathtub were filling. What the hell. Was this his lucky day or some bizarre trap? He thought back over the past few months to when it all began.

CHAPTER TWO
BIMINI

A silver dive tank clattered down the planked wooden deck, then clanged against a stanchion as the Wren heeled in a shuddering turn. The bow-pushed waves crashed against the following sea as the twin turbo engines raced to drive the vessel back to the dive site.

"I don't know. We just miscounted," Chuck muttered defensively. "I told you 25 divers was too many. You —"

"Secure that dive tank and quit your whining. It's both our butts if we can't find him. Have all the divers on a sharp lookout. If we don't find him quick I'll have to notify the Coast Guard." Angrily the Captain slouched over the wheel, his hand forcing the throttles wide open.

"Too bad we're not up in the air like that damned pelican," complained Chuck as he vainly searched the skyline. "Maybe we could see something from up there."

"Maybe yes, maybe no. No matter. The Coast Guard will put up a plane in the morning." The Captain sourly regarded his mate. "In the meantime, we better hope we find him. It ain't gonna be any fun tryin' to explain this."

The divers clung to the rails. They squinted at the darkening ocean. What would it be like. Alone. In the water. With night coming. They looked harder.

At the dive site, a grumpy brown pelican huffed away from the swirls released by the surfacing diver. Black rubber pierced the surface, followed by a facemask, mouthpiece and chin. The chin swung left, then right. At first Mark thought it must be a joke. Where the hell was the boat? It had to be somewhere close. The bastards couldn't have just left him. He scanned the murky horizon. Nothing but sky and sea. Very funny.

Again he searched the horizon. Nothing. Sixty-five-foot boats didn't just evaporate. He raised his dive mask to the top of his head. No sign of his diving buddies. Treading water, he loosened the straps on his dive tanks and weight belt. "Hell, I'm okay for now," he reassured himself, stroking the porpoise-like flexible rubber skin of his dive suit. "They'll have their big laugh, then come get me. Unless . . ."

He thought back. They anchored about three miles N.W. of Bimini. The current was flowing N.E." Lamely he struck the water. "Damn . . ." The chilled waters would take him toward the open ocean. Quickly, relentlessly. "Damn," he swore again. No point in reminding himself that the longer he went undetected the less probable his rescue.

Quickly he dismissed the dark thought. After all, they knew where he was, didn't they? Anyway, he could stay afloat for hours using the buoyancy compensator. Before then Chuck and the gang would come back. Mark took pride in his engineer's rational approach to problem-solving, even potential drowning.

The grumpy pelican returned and watched impassively from a distance. Finding nothing of interest, the bird again huffed away, skimming the surface in hopes of more interesting fare, then climbing high into the clear salt air for a better view. Seeing nothing but a noisy dive boat on the horizon, Grumpy glided on.

Mark checked his dive watch. Only one hour since he surfaced. It seemed longer. Still no ships on the horizon. He started his checklist. *No food and no fresh water, that still gives me a day, maybe more. When I see the boat I can signal them with the flash from my underwater camera.*

A wave caught him in mid-thought. Startled, he swallowed, gagging on seawater. Mark struggled to keep his face above the stinging water. *Nice move, schmuck,* he hacked, *you're in the water a few hours and already you screw-up.* The rasping salt water reminded him of just how thin was the line between death by exposure and survival. He couldn't afford many goofs. With renewed energy he continued to check his equipment. He still had a dive knife and lanyard. Otherwise, for his detection in the water he had only a whistle.

Aboard the Wren the search for Mark continued.

"There he is right over there," yelled the excited model. "See the dark head in the water!"

"Cap, over there, two points off the starboard bow." Chuck pointed.

"Okay, got him." The relieved Captain throttled back and headed toward the dark point in the water. The Wren slowed as her turbos lost their whine and black diesel smoke ebbed from the stacks. The object was now only a football field away.

"Crap." Chuck dropped his field glasses dejectedly. "It's a friggin coconut and some seaweed."

"Damn." The model, deflated by her mistake, sat down. "Damn."

Chuck moved beside her. After a reassuring pat he handed her the binoculars. "You did well seeing anything out there. It could have been him. Keep trying." She bounced back to her place on the rail and resumed her search, determined to redeem herself.

"False alarm everyone." The throttles slapped back to full and the turbos resumed their whine. Cap briefly scowled at Chuck and the girl, then resumed his heading.

"Keep lookin' he's out there somewhere." Chuck tried to sound enthusiastic. He knew the odds of finding Mark. Anyway he resumed looking.

Of this Mark knew nothing.

Anything. I'd give anything for a flare gun and some hot tea. Make that some brandy, he revised wryly. In the distance a small object appeared on the horizon. Toylike, the yacht bobbed on the surface as it moved across the ocean. Relieved, Mark flashed the camera at them and blew the whistle. Soon he'd be safe. The ship grew larger. It would only be minutes.

Soon Mark could recognize the distinctive line of a Fedship. He flashed the camera and steadily blasted out SOS on the whistle. Maybe they'd have some brandy. He smiled to himself. Better a ride home on this yacht than on the old dive boat. Mark wondered who owned the ship. He could not see anyone on deck. Something was wrong. The Fedship again seemed to be getting smaller. Impossible. The veins on Marks neck stood out as he blasted on the whistle. Frantically he waved. No one on deck. No one saw his flashes. No one heard the whistle. No one knew how close . . .

Some son of a bitch ought to make a whistle you could hear more than ten feet away. God-damned thing is useless as tits on a boar hog. Angrily he flung the whistle, then looked on foolishly as it plunged beneath the waves.

Around midnight his friend Grumpy glided back and settled with a soggy whoosh about 20 yards away. Mark wasn't certain if he simply welcomed any company or if Grumpy was starting to look like a meal, but for whatever reason he was glad to see the pelican. For a time Mark attempted to edge closer to the bird, but Grumpy always kept a respectable distance between them.

Whether overtaken by hunger or boredom, at last Grumpy again took flight, leaving Mark to watch the rising sun, alone. Mark was bone tired and he was having trouble concentrating. Chilled, he passed time thinking of ways to make heat. He'd read of POW's that had passed time and survived by similar mind games. He would survive. He'd get past the fatigue and pain.

Ouch, bitch. As the increasing swells flicked him about, he was getting battered by his own diving equipment. "You're out of here!" He yelled to the tanks after using the last of the air to fill his buoyancy compensator. He felt relieved as the jettisoned tanks dropped away into the frigid water. *Crap, if I hurt this much, those weenies at the office would be dead already.* His pride in his own physical condition was interrupted by that word. He could handle physical pain. So far that was the easy part. But anything more . . .

Until now Mark had not even allowed the possibility of the ultimate failure. Deep inside he felt a tight pressure. *No way,* he insisted. *Those ragheads couldn't kill me. No way this big pond will get my ass.*

Despite the bravado, he knew the odds of being found. Yes, he knew the odds all right. Grimacing, he removed his dive mask and scanned the horizon. With less enthusiasm he replaced the mask and searched the ocean below him. Relieved at confirming he was still alone, he returned his gaze to the surface.

Aboard the Wren they had their own problems.

"We have notified the Coast Guard," the Captain began, "and shortly a patrol boat will join us. At sunrise they will dispatch a plane to join the search. In the meantime we are continuing the search pattern and I'll appreciate your best efforts." Dejectedly he set course and prepared himself for the worst.

"Here's some hot coffee," Chuck passed the foam cups down the line of divers. "I know it's wet and uncomfortable, but we have to try. Remember, it could just as easy be any one of us out there."

Polly stumbled over to Chuck, lurched to the rail and whimpered. "I'm tired and I'm seasick and my parents will wonder where I am."

The complaint came from the Princess, as Chuck had nicknamed her. He wondered if he would be in any more trouble if he threw her spoiled ass overboard. "Just do your best," he muttered to her. "We'll be out here until he's found or we run out of fuel, so let's all make the best of this."

Polly turned and ralphed over the rail as if in reply to his encouragement. Grudgingly Chuck admitted to himself that her assessment of the situation was right on target.

Mark would have drawn little comfort from this.

You rotten bastards better find me quick, Mark raged to himself. *If you leave me here another day, I'll own that friggin boat of yours, your company, your wife, your hound dog and your bastard kids. At least I can count to twenty-five. You dumb shits can't even keep up with 25 divers.* The thought of a successful lawsuit against the boat owners temporarily lifted Mark's spirits.

But he was yanked back to the present by another sickening wrench in his gut. He felt something tugging on his swim fin and immediately imagined the worst. Sharks often brushed a target or sampled it before consuming it. *Tighten up dude, it's probably only sea weed.* Again he replaced his dive mask, stuck his head under the water and looked into the murk below. He could barely see past his swim fins.

Jesus, what did I ever do to deserve this? Unwanted answers flashed before him. He wished he hadn't asked. He wished he could change the way he'd treated Linda. Hell of a time to figure that out. He wished he hadn't disappointed his dad. Mark the dentist . . . yeah . . . right. He wished . . .Good God Almighty, he wished . . . forget it. *Dear God, please get me out of this bloody mess,* he prayed.

As he drifted he tried to estimate the tide. *Bloody hell, at three knots I could be 40 or 50 miles from the drop point. I hope Chuck can navigate better than he can count.* He decided to focus on something, anything positive. *Come on man, you got a lot going for you. You got your degree. You got a great woman. You got all the side action . . . Even though you lost the engineering job, you're still able to make a good living, something a lot of people are having a tough time doing. All in all, Bucky you're a lucky guy.*

Yeah. Sure. Who you kiddin? added his subconscious. *Lucky. Yeah. Sure. Shit.* The sky darkened. Mark checked his dive watch. Lunch time. *Lovely, simply friggin lovely.* His stomach was too empty to growl.

In mid-afternoon a sport fishing boat appeared. Mark waved. He could no longer yell because his throat was on fire, inflamed by salt spray. He tried to signal with the camera flash but nothing happened.

Five hundred dollars for you . . . you . . . piece of shit. You crap out on me . . ." He threw the camera as far as he could. He was startled. It didn't go far. *Oh crud, I'm more screwed up than I thought . . . must be hypothermia . . . screw the camera, I can get another . . .*" Mark coughed a curse from his seared lips. Salt burned his tongue and throat. The boat passed but didn't see him. He couldn't believe it. He could smell coffee being brewed and could hear the faint echo of pots from the cabin. A shiver traveled up his spine. His ears stung as if frostbitten. A septic cold crept from his forehead through his eyes. As if it were blood, he felt the cold trickle down the back of his neck.

Late in the afternoon it looked like Grumpy was returning. Mark saw a dark outline low in the sky. It grew larger. No. It was a plane. It grew larger. It was white with orange trim. Coast Guard. Thank God.

"This is Coast Guard Sierra Tango One One Nine. We're at outer marker twelve and no sign of anything. Starting turn to search sector bravo. Out." Gently the amphibian banked away and headed to cross the search path of the patrol boat.

Quiet desperation showed in the weathered features of the Captain as the Coast Guard cutter glided up beside his dive boat. A thirty-year safety record, right in the dumper. Plastering a smile on his face, he braced himself and greeted the Coast Guardsman. "Any news from the air search?" he started hopefully.

"Not a damn thing," the young officer replied. "How the heck did this happen?"

"It's started," thought the Captain, "and I'm screwed."

He was not the only one. Mark would have gladly switched places.

What bastards, deliberately ignoring me. How could they leave him? How could they just fly by? The cold poured through Mark. The pins and needles in his hands turned to branding irons. His feet were on fire. His feet were gone.

Rotten careless bastards. Shouldn't have a license if they can't see. His teeth clattered. *Imagine heat. Endless heat. Water heated. Iridescent glow.* He struggled to hold the image. A nuclear reactor. Liquid cooled. Endless heat.

Soothing — warm — blue — glowing — water.

"Here! Over Here!" he croaked. "Damn." His arms and legs felt like someone had hung dive weights on them. He knew it would be only a matter of hours before he was helpless. Now he shivered uncontrollably.

Oh God, get me out of this and I swear I'll clean up my act . . . what the hell is the matter with that asshole captain? Doesn't he know I'm missing? . . . son-of-a-bitch is probably humping the Princess, probably forgot I'm alive. Alive. The word shot through him. He could no longer feel his toes or fingers. The shivering slackened. Thoughts drifted through him effortlessly, without any seeming point of origination in his will or consciousness.

From somewhere he pulled up, *Drowning is a relatively easy and painless way to die, not much worse than freezing. God. I'd like to get my hands on the farmer that spread that manure . . . bet he never tried breathing . . . salt water . . . while his hands and feet were held down with hundred pound weights.* Mark's teeth clattered and again his body was shaken by chills.

His body seemed to be slipping away. It would be so easy to let go. Mark bit his tongue and cheeks, the pain releasing adrenaline into his flagging muscles.

Aboard the Wren everyone felt the increasing pressure as time slipped away from them.

"I'm telling you he was right there." Jabbing a spot on the map, the Captain emphasized his point.

"Well he's not there now. He's not anywhere around that spot. We've looked. The aircraft flew over it and we've sailed past it."

"Look again."

"Captain, we are continuing our search. As you well know we have about an eight percent chance of finding him, but we're still looking. I suggest you do the same. And don't plan on going too far. We'll be wanting you for an inquiry."

The Captain grunted acknowledgment. "Inquiry" sounded more like "keelhauling" to him. Damn Chuck and damn those yuppie divers anyway. Life was simpler when Papa and Phil Wylie hung out in Bimini, before the drugs and yuppies. Sport fishing and rum running, those were the days. Slowly he advanced the throttles.

Time and the ocean became the enemy for everyone.

Rage alternated with terror as Mark struggled for air. He

was freezing and drowning at the same time. "Get tough," his training commanded. *Oh, Christ*, he prayed, *get me out of this.* He struggled to keep his head upright; his neck was so tired. He was so tired. It was now about impossible to avoid breathing in the salt water. The shaking had stopped. That was bad. Fatally bad. Without consulting any training manuals he knew the next step was unconsciousness.

It's not fair, not fair, not fair . . . someone kept repeating.

"Who told you it would be fair?" shouted his father. Wearily Mark lifted his head, struggling to turn slightly, half expecting to see his dad. He was not there. No one was there, only a boat. A boat?

He struggled to focus. *The turkey can't be 400 meters away, what is he, blind? Thank God the dude in the tower looks like he sees me . . . Wake up, you idiot . . . All right! Here! Here! Thank you Jesus!* He giggled, shivered, tried to wave, but could not.

The skipper, spotting Mark in the water, throttled the engine back. As the big diesel slowed, the exhaust thickened and drifted with the boat. The fumes reached Mark just before the boat and he was overcome with nausea. The fire in his throat poured down into his gut, but he was too weak to vomit.

The rotten bastard was trying to poison him. *Help me, you son of a —* As the boat approached, dimly Mark saw a large man move to the side and yell to another. "Lower the diving ladder! Then be ready with the man overboard ring."

In the three-foot swells it was difficult to maneuver. Mark tried to extend to his full six-foot-three-inch length and prayed for enough strength to grip the rescue ring. He could not. The large man reached over the rail with a long hook, grabbed Mark over the shoulder, then pulled him to the dive ladder. As he reached for the ship's rail, strong hands grabbed him.

So came Lazarus, back from the grave, he thought wearily.

The big man lifted him onto the deck, then turned to his companion and ordered, "Treat him for hypothermia while I notify the Coast Guard."

Looking back at Mark, he asked, "What's your name, bud?"

"Mark," he managed hoarsely. Another great effort produced a raspy, "Hansen."

"I'm Paul Reynolds, and you're aboard the Happy Camper." The large man advanced the throttle and the engine revved. Mark felt the ship pulsating as it lurched into a turn. The skipper used the radio, set some switches, and disappeared into the cabin.

The mate bundled Mark in a wool blanket and started rubbing his hands and feet. Paul reappeared from the cabin with two mugs.

"Warm him from the inside out," Paul directed the mate.

After several mugs of hot coffee and a boost with some Courvasier, Mark was finally able to speak. "Do me a favor," he croaked, "Radio Bimini and let the morons know I'm okay."

As the mate worked on his feet, the captain, a huge Floridian, told Mark the rescue story. "We heard some idiot, no offense, had gotten separated from a dive party. But you're not where they said you'd be." Paul shook his head. "You are one lucky mother. I wasn't looking for you. Frankly we just plain stumbled across you in the water."

Mark grunted an acknowledgment. He hurt all over, but especially where the straps for the dive tank and weight belts had crossed over his body.

Paul reached over and put a cushion under Mark's head. "You know, I was stranded at sea once." He shivered slightly, as he recalled his own horror story. "In my case, we weren't SCUBA diving, we'd been doing shrimp research and I got separated from the lab ship."

Paul's husky voice trailed off. His eyes clouded over. "I must have seen five other ships and planes passing, but they never saw me." He made a sweeping motion with his hand, mimicking the planes and boats. "I had a signal mirror as well as smoke flares. Even so, it was just dumb luck that some kids out fishing in a Boston Whaler found me before the boys in the gray suits got me."

Abruptly Paul rose and checked his compass. He had set course for South Bimini and then the fishing docks. "You know we're both lucky mothers." Paul turned and smiled grimly at Mark. "We lose more than 300 sailors a year just from the U. S. commercial fishing fleets — and who knows how many civilians."

Mark nodded without speaking. Again the water rushed over him. Suddenly his hands and feet tingled. The gagging smell of diesel fumes rushed back. Paul's voice jolted him back to the safety of the Happy Camper as another wave of nausea rolled over him.

"Anyway, by the time they've turned around, the poor devil has two chances, slim and none. It's even worse when they lose a guy off a nuclear sub."

"Whoa." Mark cocked his head, one eyebrow lifting. "Off a sub?"

"Sure. You don't think they really stay down all the time. They surface for unloading agents or recovering them — and for dropping off and recovering equipment and electronic packages." Mark wondered how Paul knew that.

"Just last year we lost three guys off the deck of a nukie sub in Japanese waters and the press got hold of it. Either the press didn't understand what was going on or someone got to them, because nothing was made of it. But I understand it happens all the time, because the decks of subs aren't flat — and they sure aren't made for taking a stroll." A shrug and a shake of his head concluded Paul's commentary.

Mark frowned thoughtfully, "I'm an electronic engineer by training —although I'm doing something else now — I'd think it would be easy enough to put a radio transmitter on these Navy guys so they could be found." Mark gestured a small package and moved his hand to his left shoulder as if attaching the radio to his tank straps.

The spiked coffee was starting to work. A surge of warmth flushed over him. Why not? he thought smugly.

Paul shuffled his feet impatiently and smirked tolerantly as the young man gestured. He paused thoughtfully, then explained. "It just isn't that simple, Mark. In the first place, a lot of the time they're on radio silence and they simply cannot allow any active electronic signals." He slumped into a chair.

Mark nodded. "Makes sense."

Paul paused and drew a deep breath. "But there's more to it than that. Even if the guy has a transmitter, you can only narrow the search to a half mile or so at best."

Mark shivered again as he pictured ships passing closer than that, seeing nothing.

"You saw today, that doesn't get the job done, even in three-foot swells. Imagine eight-foot or thirty-foot waves. No, they need something better, but I don't know what." Paul shook his head.

You may not know, but I think I do, Mark thought excitedly. *I know, by God, I know!* Silently he reveled in the knowledge.

Paul tilted his Budweiser and savored his beer. Then eyeing Mark curiously he asked, "Anyway, what the heck is an electronic engineer doing in Bimini all by himself?"

"Well, right now this engineer isn't engineering." Mark shrugged. "The company I worked for ate it and died when a Taiwan outfit made a cheap copy of our main product line, so I've been keeping groceries on the table by doing some other stuff."

Paul put down his beer, then prodded, "Look Mark, why so mysterious? Hell, half the troops here in the islands are running dope or guns or illegal aliens. No one gives a shit what you do."

Mark softened. A smile slowly spread over his youthful features. " No. I'm afraid it's nothing that exciting. I do fashion modeling and catalogs, commercials and stuff. And you know what everyone says about male models. I just don't like to be painted with that brush, you know."

Paul let out a sound like a bottlenose dolphin blowing. Beer splashed from his mouth and nose as he convulsed with laughter. "You mean you'd rather be thought of as a thief or doper than a model."

"In Lauderdale a young single guy is better off being

thought of as a thief than a male model," retorted Mark.

Paul nodded.

The conversation drifted from ships to women. Over the last of the Budweiser and Courvasier Paul waxed philosophical: "And if you stood 'llem all on their heads they'd all be alike anyway."

On that happy thought, Mark fell asleep. Every now and then, however, as the boat plodded back toward port, his body twitched when murky images of hammerhead sharks and water-filled lungs intruded upon his rest.

CHAPTER THREE
THE IDEA

After agreeing to get together down in Islamorada, Mark thanked Paul for his help, then prepared to return to Ft. Lauderdale, refusing Paul's offer to take him by boat.

"Thanks, but I'm not ready to get back on a boat just yet," Mark grinned. "A friend of mine is going to pick me up at the airfield. Anyway, I appreciate the offer." Mark added to himself, and I'm not going to tempt fate by taking one of those elderly island hoppers back to the mainland. Fred Stephens, a photographer friend from Palm Beach who was a private pilot, had agreed to pick him up.

For a dead man, I feel great, he thought, as he waited near the customs shack for his friend to come in with his Cessna. Mark watched a small white airplane approaching. A strange looking craft, it looked like it was flying backwards. As the plane came closer Mark saw that it was even tinier than he thought and it was indeed flying backwards. He scanned the sky for Fred's familiar Cessna 210, but saw nothing.

He moved his toes in the borrowed Reeboks. Even toe wiggling feels good, he reflected. After yesterday, I'm damned lucky I can even feel 'em. The sun's heat on his face and arms felt good. Not good, great.

The small white plane had taxied over and shut down.

The canopy was opening. Mark wished it hadn't. It was Fred. A small handsome man, fiftyish in appearance, his hair white and close cropped military style, hopped out of the cockpit. He strode over to his friend, shook his hand and steered him toward the airplane. "Hey Dude, how do you like my new wings?"

"Great Fred, but how are we getting back to Lauderdale?" Skeptically, Mark appraised the airplane.

"Come on, Mark, there's room in there, you just can't bring your dive tanks. They'll have to come over later." Grinning broadly, Fred motioned to the rear seat of the plane. Later he would learn why that was not a problem.

Mark looked in, still dubious. As his hand rested on the body of the plane he was surprised to find that it felt like the smooth rubber of his wet suit. He looked at Fred quizzically.

Fred was enjoying Mark's obvious admiration of his latest toy. He could see wheels spinning in the young engineer's mind. Billy, his only son, used to get that same look. That was before he was . . . before he . . . Fred hit the plane with his fist, then stroked it proudly. "Fiberglass and carbon fibre composite. It's stronger and lighter than steel and nearly invisible to radar." He paused, looking back at Mark, who had tightened noticeably. "Don't worry, we have a transponder so the air traffic controllers can keep track of us."

Reluctantly Mark coiled his six-foot-three hulk into the rear seat. The airplane was roomier than it appeared from the outside. It was almost comfortable, if one forgot it was homebuilt and flew backwards. As his friend Sean Knight said, "Don't let nothing but fear hold you back." Anyway, Mark couldn't weenie out on Fred, of all people. He'd never live it down.

Paul said yesterday that I'd rather be thought a thief than a model, he reminded himself. Well, I guess I'd rather die in this damned plane than be thought a coward. Anyway, it couldn't be my time to bite the big one. If it were, that would have happened in the water yesterday. What the hell, maybe I've got a second chance for a good reason . . . He buckled the shoulder harness extra tight.

As Fred guided the Vari-Eze toward the mainland, Mark

attempted to tell him about his narrow escape. "It was strange. At first I wasn't worried, just pissed off. But when it got a little hairy, I realized I might not make it. It sort of got me thinking."

"That must have been a new experience," said Fred dryly. It wasn't meant unkindly, but just slipped out. As much as he liked Mark, Fred had already learned that his young friend never took anything seriously; not his job, not his family, not . . .

Another time Mark might have taken offense, but now he understood, reached forward and gently punched Fred on the shoulder, interrupting the older man's reverie.

"Thanks a lot," he said, "but I am serious. It was, let's say, attention-getting out there. You know I haven't been straight with Linda, I've been with some other girls. It never bothered me before, but it bothered me out there. I realized how I felt about her. And I thought about my dad . . . but mostly I guess I just got mad at myself."

Fred swallowed hard and almost turned around to look at Mark. He did sound serious. Maybe — at last, this dunk in the ocean had really given him a mental kick-start.

"So why are you mad at yourself?" He adjusted the throttle and waited for a reply.

"Well, I think maybe I haven't been doing much with what I've been given, you know." Mark flinched internally. It hurt to admit that to himself, much less to Fred.

Amen, thought Fred. Out loud he added, "So what are you going to do?"

"The first thing is tell Linda how I really feel about her."

"You sure this isn't just a guilt trip and pity party you're going on?"

"Now that's cold, Fred. Give me a break, will you?" He fell silent a moment, and when he spoke again, Fred realized from the tone of his voice he wasn't playing games. "No, I honestly did some soul searching . . . about a lot of things. I finally decided what I'm going to do with my life, at least for a while." He looked out over the water, seeing much further.

"This conversation is getting too heavy for an aircraft intercom. Let's stop at the Aero Squadron for some lunch and you can tell me the whole thing." Fred started his approach to the airfield. He was curious to hear more.

He flew into Oceanside airport off Powerline Road in Pompano Beach. For a time Oceanside had been favored by dopers, but a series of sting operations and arrests had toned that down. As law enforcement had been strengthened, the drug dealers shifted South toward the Keys and North toward Orlando in the middle of the state. Fred liked the informal atmosphere at Oceanside. It sure beat the heck out of the International Airport.

"I have a hangar at the North side of the field now," he told Mark. "I still have the Cessna in Palm Beach, but this is more fun." He taxied the plane to the parking area and shut down.

They strolled toward the restaurant. A chubby burrowing owl glared at them as they passed his perch on the wooden fence that separated the airfield from the parking area. "Damn bird always critiques my landings," Fred smirked.

The Aero Squadron was decorated like a WWII British pub. Pieces of WWII airplanes hung from the ceiling and outside were trucks, guns and paraphernalia from the war. Several times a year veterans would fly to the airport in Mustangs, Thunderbolts and even a Flying Fortress. They would eat, drink and celebrate. That war, like all wars, looked much better from a distance.

The entrance was dark. As Fred's eyes adjusted to the light he recognized April, the hostess. Without asking, she smiled graciously and led them to a table in the nonsmoking section near the window overlooking the runway. Everyone remembers a good tipper.

Fred and Mark were comfortably seated. Mark scanned the menu. His eye stopped on Seafood. "I'll have the Shrimp Louis," he said to the waitress.

Fred grinned at him, shook his head. "Make that two."

"I would have thought you'd had enough of anything to do with the ocean after your deep dip in the big pond." He was still shaking his head.

They both decided on beer with a twist of lime.

"As you were saying about the future," Fred continued as he moved a butter dish and arranged his silverware.

"You know Fred, since yesterday I've been thinking about what almost happened to me. I have some ideas. But I need a mechanical engineer and maybe a chemist."

Mark had been gazing at the wing of a British Spitfire, but now turned to Fred.

"Go on," said Fred.

"I think I have a way to find people when they get separated from their dive boats and maybe even more than that. I think it would work to find anyone overboard or pilots down at sea or even life rafts or whatever, anything in the water you need to find."

"The military should love it." Fred rearranged his silverware, cleared his throat, and smiled at Mark. He was surprised at his apparent naivete. "Mark I don't want to burst your bubble, but they already make stuff like that. There's a big company in Lauderdale that makes emergency position indicators, you know EPIRBS. They have a battery and send a signal and the Coast Guard comes to get you," he snapped his fingers, "just like that."

"That's what I thought too, Fred, but I was talking to Paul Reynolds, the skipper of the Happy Camper, and he tells me that the EPIRBS don't work half the time because the batteries die in the salt water."

Fred sat back in his chair. He was enjoying his friend's animation.

"Worse yet," Mark continued, "they work when you don't want them to and send the Coast Guard on wild goose chases. The Coast Guard hates that. Even when the EPIRBS do work they don't help anyone pinpoint the victims or survivors."

Fred raised his eyebrows. Mark not only seemed to have a good idea, but he seemed to be cranked up enough to go to bat for it. He was pleased but at the same time skeptical.

"Okay," he drawled, "say you have an idea and maybe it'll even work. You don't know jack shit about business. No offense, Mark. What about a patent? Where are you going to get the money? And how are you going to sell it? "

He paused and closely observed the impact of his words. His young friend appeared undeterred. "I don't want to be rude but you're just barely covering the payments on the Explorer and your bar tabs at Shooters. How do you think you're going to be able to design or develop your idea, much less manufacture it or market it?"

Again Fred paused to read Mark's response. He seemed undaunted, so Fred hit the point again. "You know I went through this when I invented that audio indicator for portable battery packs for photographers. I've got a feeling you're talking something much more complicated and expensive than that. You might be looking at a half million or more."

Fred eased back in his seat to allow his mini-lecture to sink in. Although he felt obliged to be honest with Mark, at the same time he didn't want to squelch his enthusiasm. More than anything he wanted his young friend to move on with his life — and maybe he really did mean business. Fred waited.

Mark eyed Fred squarely. His jaw was set. "Look Fred, I know you're trying to be a good friend. But I think I've got a really great idea that can save lives. I know there must be some way to raise the money and get the help I need to market it." Fred was quietly amused. If Mark had been a cartoon character, smoke would have been pouring from his ears. His eyes were smoldering.

"Just because I'm doing modeling work doesn't mean I'm an airhead." He stabbed at his salad, as if to emphasize his point. "Anyway I've seen enough American ideas wind up becoming Japanese or Hong Kong companies. I'm going to do this somehow, and I'd appreciate any help you can give. But with or without, I'm going to do this."

Mark was wound up tight. Fred saw his knuckles whiten as he gripped the knife and removed it from the salad.

"Hang on, friend, I'm too young to die in a restaurant brawl." Fred backed away in mock fright.

Mark looked down and realized how foolish he must look, gripping the dinner knife. He half regretted the way he talked to Fred, but he didn't at all regret what he'd said.

"Yeah, and I'm too handsome to fry for doing an old buzzard like you," he grinned, mostly at himself.

This was more than Fred expected. He leaned forward, smiling faintly. "Hey slow down, pard, I wasn't trying to bust your chops, I've just seen a lot of inventors with great ideas wind up in the dumpster. The standing joke at Sandia is there are hundreds of great technologies looking for a problem." Fred also knew that most of them were better prepared in business and better set financially; and maybe a lot brighter than Mark. He looked at him intently. Mark was not backing down. Fred could feel his resistance and he liked it.

Mark's posture remained rigid, softened only by the last traces of his disappearing grin.

Finally, Fred straightened his shoulders, inhaled deeply, and said, "If you're really that serious, I think you should first talk to my patent attorney. You'll probably find out that your idea is not as original as you think, or there are good reasons that such a product is not already being made."

Fred wished he could give Mark a capsule business education. There was so much he had to learn. "There's one other thing I don't think you understand, Mark. Even if you do have a valid idea that can be patented, that still doesn't mean it'll make money. You say it will save lives, that's fine, but that won't get you a dime of investment money." He squeezed his fingers together a few inches in front of Mark's nose. "If you can't convince potential investors that this will earn more money for them than they would make with their funds safely in T-Bills or IBM stock, you can forget it. They are looking for obscene profits. How much money do you figure you need?"

Frankly, I don't know, yet." Mark pushed his salad away.

Fred sighed openly. "Mark I don't want to be cruel, but you . . ." He paused, noting the wounded look in Mark's eyes. He searched for the right words to soften, but only slightly, what had to be said. "Granted you might luck into some tuna that will back you for the good of mankind, but I wouldn't bet the farm on that happening. Understand one more thing. This is business."

"Fred, I appreciate what you're telling me. I don't think I

need a patent attorney yet. Hell, so far it's just an idea."

Ah, again the naivete shows, thought the older man. "That's what I was just trying to tell you, Mark. This is business. Dammit, forget friendship, forget common sense, and just remember this is business. Remember the Godfather, for crying out loud. Remember what happened to your former employer."

Fred paused, grappling for a way to wise-up his young friend without insulting him. "If you discuss your idea with anyone before you protect it, you may wake up to find that you can't, because it's already been published." Fred hesitated, then added, "Worse than that, you may find your idea becoming a product made by the friend you discussed it with."

To emphasize the point he added, "I don't even want you to tell me any more about your idea until you talk to Ordean Jacobs. He specializes in patent law."

"Okay, I give up." Mark raised his hands in surrender. "Give me Jacob's number when you get back to your office. But I have another mission I must complete." Sheepishly he glanced at his watch. "If I don't get together with Linda I'm in deep kimshi. Besides she sounded really worried about me when I called to tell her I was all right. If you'll drop me off where I can get my car, I'll call you later and get that number."

Fred studied Mark's expression. There was something in his eyes. As a photographer he was a pro. Never had he seen such intensity and determination in youthful eyes. This was a different Mark. A week ago the kid wouldn't have had a mature concern for anyone.

Fred pushed back from the table and put a fatherly arm on Mark's shoulder, gently shaking him, "Okay, son. Just remember, you may know electronics and you may be developing a name in modeling, but you'll get eaten alive if you don't stay awake on this one."

The two friends walked to the parking lot of the restaurant. They approached a bright metallic green Mercedes 500 SL.

"How do you like it?" Fred asked casually.

"What's not to like?" replied Mark. Then he realized this was another of Fred's toys. If it were not electronics, it was boats.

If not boats, planes. Many times Mark wondered privately how he did it. A photographer . . . Again he wondered, but he would never come out and ask. Besides, he had something more important on his mind.

CHAPTER FOUR
TO BE DESIRED

"Hi Ordean, this is Fred. A friend of mine named Mark Hansen is going to call you. He has an idea for some kind of an emergency location device." Fred rested his feet on the desktop. "Do me a favor. He's a kid, but he's good people. He doesn't have much business sense yet, but I'd appreciate any help you can give him. He has potential. He's just too trusting for his own good and I think he's going to need you."

Fred leaned back and sank deeper in his chair, "If necessary, I'll guarantee his bill up to $15,000 but please don't say anything to him about it, okay?" He hesitated, waiting for Ordean's response.

Ordean listened quietly, debated a moment, then cautiously proceeded. "Look Fred, I'll be glad to help this young man for you, but tell me one thing, is this another kid who reminds you of Billy?"

Abruptly Fred dropped his feet to the floor and sat erect in his chair. He knew that his friend meant well and was only looking out for his best interests.

"Thanks Ordean," he said curtly, "but he is a good kid and I have to do this. If I'm wrong, do us both a favor — don't say I told you so."

Ordean was right of course, Mark did remind him of Billy,

who'd died in Lebanon. He gazed long and hard at the gold-framed photograph on his desk. His twelfth birthday. His first camera. That expression. Such a good-looking talented kid. So sensitive, such an eye for pattern and texture. He would have been a great photographer, a great . . . His eyes misted. He looked away from the photograph. Why couldn't he put it somewhere so he didn't have to look at it? Even the trip to the Mideast had done nothing more than temporarily relieve the anguish. *Aw, screw it. They're only loaned to us anyway, and I had him longer than some people.*

Unsuccessfully he tried to tighten himself up. Maybe Mark was a surrogate son or maybe he was just a nice kid he wanted to help. What did it matter? Fred knew he would give Mark the boost he needed. That was that.

Mark pulled into a parking space at Tugboat's. As he strolled toward the entrance, he noticed a blue heron gulping down a small fish from the shallows of the waterway. "Braver than I am," he heckled the bird, "I wouldn't eat anything out of that cruddy water."

He quickened his pace. Mark longed to see Linda more than he understood. For the first time he questioned his feelings. "She's not the best looking girl I ever dated. Sure, she can hold her own with any twelve candidates from the calendar of your choice . . . and her brown hair, lightened by the South Florida sun, looks and smells like honey . . ." He stopped, feeling foolish. But the thoughts forced their way back.

Maybe Fred was right, thoughts are virgin where I'm concerned. Naahhh." Self-effacement was not in his repertoire.

He explored further. Was it the way she treated him or just that she was the one near him now? No, it was more than that. Maybe it just boiled down to who she was. *Hell maybe it just doesn't matter . . . We feel how we feel and that's it . . .*

Tugboat's was located on the Intercoastal waterway right off U. S. Highway l, near several marinas and shipyards, so it attracted an interesting assortment of people. Yard workers, ship owners, bikini bunnies, groupies and assorted singles on the make all found it a welcome haven.

Linda was already seated at the outdoor bar by the boat dock. Mark saw her and stopped. "Have I changed so much?" he wondered. Was he so nearsighted before? In a white bathing suit covered by a print skirt, she was arresting.

Brushing past some patrons, he hurried to the bar. Linda spotted him and turned on the barstool. Mark slipped his hands around her waist and pulled and lifted her toward him. Silently, she clasped her hands behind his neck.

"Damn, I'm so glad to see you sugar," he whispered.

Linda stroked his cheek, then lightly kissed him on the mouth. She relaxed in his arms. "Let's look at you. See what the seabirds dragged in." What she saw chilled and excited her. He looked older, or maybe it was just the weathered look from exposure. No — it seemed much more; an intensity in those wonderful green eyes she had never seen before. When she looked at him it was as if she could see through them clear into the ocean. Quickly she closed her own eyes. She saw something in the depths that frightened her.

"Jeez, do I look that beat up?" he chided her.

"No hon, you look fine, for driftwood that is." She nuzzled him and relaxed her grip behind his neck, mentioning nothing of her vision.

Mark replaced her on the stool and settled next to her. As he sat down, Annette, a newer waitress, eased over to take his order.

"I'll have the Long Island Ice Tea." He turned his head toward Linda, "And for the lady?"

"That sounds good." Linda was disappointed that she wasn't asked for I.D. As a senior at the University of Miami she was now 21, the legal drinking age. Before now, every place she went wanted to see her I.D. Maybe they could tell.

"So . . . How's the aquaculture class?"

Linda grinned and brushed the question aside. "Is that what you really want to talk about?"

"No," he blushed, "much more important things." He seemed to draw energy from her.

She fidgeted in her chair. "Maybe someplace a little more

private?"

Mark nodded. "Forget the drinks," he called to Annette, slipping some money on the bar.

Linda hopped off the stool and headed toward the door. Her leather sandals made a slight clipping sound as she moved, and her bottom jiggled delightfully.

"Damn, she is fine," he thought.

She glanced back at him. What was that look on her face? He'd never seen that expression before. A slight push of salty air carried her fragrance toward him. Her movements seemed to be slowed as if in stop action photography. She paused, turned, reached up with her right hand and placed it behind his neck, drawing his head down to hers.

"Will you take me home?" She spoke so softly he wasn't certain he heard her correctly.

"Home. Coconut Grove?" he asked, his chest tightening.

She nodded.

As soon as they hit I-95 South they got caught in the usual traffic jam.

"Looks like a long ride," Mark muttered.

"It's okay, we're in no hurry," she lied, reaching over and gently resting her hand on his arm.

"Right." He smiled, enjoying her caress.

Screw it, it was worth a ticket. He pressed harder on the accelerator, hurried through the flow of traffic past the International airport, past County Line Road and then to Coconut Grove.

They parked in front of Linda's building and silently raced up the concrete staircase to her second floor apartment. Linda hurriedly unlocked the door.

"Why don't you get us something to drink?" she called over her shoulder as she pushed open the door and headed toward the bath adjoining the bedroom.

In the kitchen Mark found a bottle of Mateus in the refrigerator.

"Is wine all right?" Receiving no reply, he removed the cork and took two glasses with him to the bedroom. His eyes traveled to the bathroom door. It was ajar.

Funny, he'd often daydreamed of this and in his mind's eye he always pictured Dom Perignon Champagne on a sailboat or maybe at a ski lodge; preceded by much conversation and maneuvering — followed by a demure and reluctant acceptance. Instead, Linda had been the initiator. Mark mused upon the unexpected events of the past days as he absently stared out the window at a sleek sailboat gliding into the harbor. Someday they'd have a sailboat like that.

Mark heard the water running in the oversize Jacuzzi and knew that Linda had slipped out of the skirt and bathing suit and was preparing herself for him.

He poured wine in both glasses and moved silently to the tantalizing bathroom door. Had she deliberately done that? He waited. Almost certainly. Even so he was not prepared for the vision that met him when he stole a look through the narrow opening.

Mark had seen dozens of women without their clothing. He had seen dozens of fine-looking women without their clothing. He had seen dozens of fine looking models without their clothing. But still, he was not prepared.

She was standing in the tub, looking right through him. Although motionless she generated the feeling of movement, no, of acceleration. If I drowned and this is a dream, don't let me wake up, Mark prayed.

In a single motion she raised her arm and twisted her wrist so that at first her palm faced him. Then she withdrew it to herself, compelling him to open the door. He watched her settle into the Jacuzzi with the grace of a gardenia petal drifting upon the water.

Quickly he removed his shoes, shirt and trunks.

Linda had started the water jets in the tub. The expression on her face told Mark there was nothing he could do wrong. He moved into the tub with her.

Ironic, he thought, as he pulled Linda to him in the swirling water. Ironic, that in water he had been in terror and nearly lost his life, and now in water he was in love and was finding it.

Mark reached for the wine from beside the tub. Deftly he

placed a glass in Linda's hand.

"Love, Life, and Happiness," he toasted. They sipped lightly, then replaced the goblets on the base beside the tub.

"I love you, Linda," he laughed as he ran his wine-chilled finger down her cheek.

"Me too," she answered, mischievously starting all over again. Appreciatively she watched as he exited the tub and dried himself.

"Me too," she repeated as she joined him beside the tub.

Wonderfully warm and relaxed, they sipped a final toast and slipped beneath the covers. "After you pick the date you should tell your mom and dad," he murmured. "They'll want to make plans too."

"Pick what date?" she impishly replied.

Mark propped up on one elbow. "Oh, I see. You'll have your way with me and then I'm yesterday's newspaper."

"My brother always said it was silly to buy the cow if . . ."

Mark interrupted her with a kiss.

"Different rules for bulls," he grinned, "A good bull is hard to . . ."

"Chauvinist." She reached under the covers and grabbed his attention.

"You cheat." He pulled her to him.

"My house, my rules." Linda nipped at his ear.

"Best two falls out of three?" Mark trailed a finger down her spine.

Linda simply nodded, "Ummm. Maybe I should call mom tonight."

"Tomorrow." He traced the outline of her collarbone with his finger. "After breakfast."

"Ummmm."

CHAPTER FIVE
TRUE BELIEVERS

"I'm just no good at love out loud." The words to the song ran through Mark's mind. He rolled over on his side and looked at Linda, who was still sleeping peacefully. He was experiencing an uncommon mixture of feelings toward her, something unexpected and life-altering — different, the way he felt this morning from the way he'd felt the other times.

Everything seemed to be fitting together. Linda – love — life. A future with a plan, worthwhile ideas. God, he felt great. He knew his ideas were original. He didn't care what Fred thought. Mentally he scanned the catalogs he'd read. He was certain the locator was original; he'd never seen any product like it. For this project he was ready. But, the big project . . . he wasn't ready . . . yet . . . on that, he needed help so, it would have to wait.

He wanted to meet Sean at the hobby shop and share the locator idea with him. Then he would talk to Ordean.

Linda woke and briefly cuddled next to him. "Where are we this morning?" she chided him.

"Sorry sugar. I was just thinking about my meeting with Fred yesterday. You know, I think I've really hit something with my idea for an emergency locator." He pulled her closer, teasing her hair, speaking softly. "When I nearly . . . uhm . . . when I was in Bimini, I got the idea for a way to find sailors lost at sea. Fred wants me to see his patent attorney and I want to talk to Sean about it."

Linda propped up on one elbow, intently studying her lover. "That sounds like a marvelous idea. Tell me how it works."

"I haven't got all the details worked out, but basically it is a radar reflecting balloon that can be seen for miles. Divers and boaters would carry one in a little pouch on their life jacket."

"Maybe I'm a little prejudiced, but it sounds like a terrific idea to me." She moved closer to him, lightly kissing his cheek.

Again he stroked her hair. "Strange how a close call can really open your eyes." Gently he kissed her.

"Yes," she said, "it makes you think about what's important to you . . ." she hesitated, " . . . who's really important to you."

"Right both times," he whispered, pulling her to him.

"So when do you have to see the patent person?" She looked up invitingly.

"Later."

Later that morning Mark dressed and headed toward Fort Lauderdale. Linda gazed from the bedroom window at the harbor. She smiled at her reflection in the glass. *Good morning, Mrs. Mark Hansen!* Her thoughts were interrupted by the phone. It was Daphne Leland, her best friend from school.

"I hope I didn't wake you, but I really need to talk with you." She sounded tense.

"Well, it must be fate, Dee because I want to talk to you, too. What's up?"

"Let's meet at the Lakeside Coffee Shop," Daphne suggested.

"Okay. How about after computer class, about 11?"

"Deal."

As Linda drove up, Daphne was just ahead of her, parking her red convertible. The tall, attractive girl was wearing a school sweatshirt and long pants. Her close-cropped hair was fluffed from the wind.

After they went through the cafeteria line they settled at a table by the lake. A large black swan was gliding past. Majestic.

Dominating the lake. Linda turned to her friend to speak, but paused. Linda was concerned by Daphne's expression. "Hey, friend, you look troubled," she ventured. "What's wrong?"

"You've met Peter Worden," said Daphne, "and I suppose you figured out that he and I have gotten, well, very close over the past semester."

Indeed Linda knew Peter Worden. She did not like him. There was something false about him that reminded her of snakes, or spiders. And yes, she'd figured out that Daphne and Peter were on intimate terms.

"I know Peter," she said. *Oh God,* she panicked, *he's gotten her pregnant or infected her with some yucky disease, the bastard.* "What happened?"

"I caught him with another girl. Saturday I was shopping and I just dropped over to his apartment." Daphne's gaze shifted to the ground. "I never thought of calling him first. Maybe I should have called. Maybe I'm glad I didn't. Anyway, he came to the door in his bathing suit when I rang the bell. I could see right past him. The back side of a girl was slipping from the living room toward the bathroom." Her voice trembled and broke and the muscles in her face tightened as she relived the experience.

"She had her clothing in her hand, not on her big wiggling ass. I was so hurt and pissed-off, I couldn't decide whether to yell or cry or laugh. I ended up yelling. I mean seriously loud." Again her voice broke.

Angrily Linda watched her friend struggle against the tears. It was too bad Daphne hadn't drop-kicked his manly pride over the living room table.

"Listen Daphne. Thank God — I mean, that you know the kind of person he is. That you found out before it was too late. And it's not, well you know, another problem —"

"Of course, you're right." Daphne nodded, pulling a tissue and blowing her nose. "Look, Linda, I know Peter was never your favorite person, but I really enjoyed being with him. I saw he had some faults, but he was so sweet when we were alone. And he was sort of special under certain circumstances, you know." She tilted her head and her cheeks flushed.

Damn. Why did so many women gravitate to guys who mistreated them? Sick, but true. Of course there are exceptions like Mark. Linda smiled.

Daphne stared quizzically at her. "What are you smiling about? I just got dumped on by my boyfriend. Is that somehow humorous? Am I missing the joke?"

"I'm sorry," Linda apologized, "but I was thinking about the difference between Mark and Peter and I know it is terrible to compare . . ."

Daphne silently listened. Although Mark was very handsome she had never been impressed by the way he treated Linda. Granted, he had animal magnetism. And anyway, the two men were not comparable.

Acknowledging the polite silence, Linda demurred, "Don't let me interrupt what you were saying. It's true that I didn't really care for Peter. It's just that I thought you deserved someone much better." She weighed her words carefully. "You have too much talent, and you're too smart – and too attractive, to put up with the way he treats you. I just never felt I should say anything. I mean, who am I to tell you who to date? I'm not your mom."

Daphne reached over and hugged Linda. "You may not be my mom, but you certainly are my sister. And you can say what's on your mind anytime. It's just that I know Peter can be a rat but he can be so wonderful. He apologized and promised he'd never do anything like that again if I would just forgive him. He even made the other girl leave."

"And?" Linda smiled at her friend and watched, already knowing what she was going to say.

"Oh, he seemed so sincere, I just don't know what to do. I don't know whether to give him a second chance or what. I mean, we're not engaged or anything but I thought we had an understanding. I can't believe he would do something like that." She stared into the black water of the lake.

What Daphne had not told Linda was that her monthly had been late and she'd been picturing what would've happened if she were pregnant and had discovered Peter with another woman. "I feel so betrayed." She reached over and touched Linda's hand, "I guess it's just difficult to deal with alone. I'm grateful to be able to dump this on you, Linda. Thank you. Believe me, I feel lucky to have you as a friend."

Linda thought quietly for a few moments. "Dee, I wouldn't presume to tell you what you should do. Anyway, I know I'm prejudiced when it comes to Peter. When I was stumped and couldn't decide what to do, my dad used to tell me to get out a piece of paper and write a letter to him or mom with the pros and cons, and ask them for advice. Then I was to pretend to be one of them and to answer my own letter."

"You know what?" Daphne shook her head. "I've already done that. A teacher taught me that technique. It's been helpful in the past, but this time – this time, it's not working. I guess there's really only one problem." She smiled at Linda through her tears. "I know what I should do. I should tell him to get stuffed, but I already know I'm going to give him a second chance.Oh, men!" Oh men . . . she repeated to herself. What was Peter's hold on her, anyway? "So everything is good with you and Mark?"

"Very," exclaimed Linda radiantly. "Very very! I want you two to get to know each other better."

"Isn't this sudden?" *Strange,* thought Daphne. *I thought Peter was the constant one and Mark the playboy. Just goes to show . . . what? What —?* All along she'd been worried not about herself, but about Linda getting hurt! "I mean, when you say 'very, very' do you mean VERY VERY?"

Linda nodded, grinning shyly.

"Oh, Linda! I'm so happy for you!" Daphne jumped up and gave her a hug. "God, love is great, isn't it?"

"It's okay until something better comes along." Linda returned her friend's hug, but her thoughts were with Mark.

A massive Purple Grackle loudly scolded Mark as he patiently waited for the two riders to cross College Avenue. One of the horses hesitated, and whinnied at the bird as if in reprimand for breaking the morning silence. Mark thought how different was Davie from the rest of Lauderdale, much as Sean was different from other people Mark knew.

Mark knew Fred had cautioned him to be careful about telling anyone his idea, but Sean Knight was the perfect one to use as a sounding board. Besides, Linda thought he was a straight up person and her intuition was rarely off center. Mark had met Sean playing amateur soccer, and later they'd shared an interest in experimental science. Despite the twenty-year age difference, Sean could hold his own on the field. A mutual respect had matured.

As he continued down College Avenue past Saturn University on his way to Sean's hobby store in Davie, Mark was now reminded of his first meeting with Fred. At the time, he was a student at Saturn. A professor had introduced them; Fred was teaching graduate school as an adjunct in International Marketing or something. Strange . . . but fortunate.

Mark pulled up and parked in front of Sean's store, located in an earth-tone two-story masonry building. The natural wood trim work and Western accents, including a hitching rail, so typical of the little town, would make a great backdrop for photographic work, but the store exterior certainly belied the high-tech nature of Sean's Hobbies. Sean had specialized in remote control airplanes, helicopters and boats for several years following the theft of his fishing business in Jamaica by the Manley pirates. He'd been lucky to get out of the country with his life, but he had friends, including a school teacher, who hadn't made it.

"Good day Sandy, how's my girl?" Mark tossed a greeting to a pudgy black Labrador peeking out from behind the counter.

"Woof!"

A second greeting came from the back of the store. "Hi, Mark. Sean's upstairs, go on up." Barbara, Sean's wife, was busy with a customer. She waved as he went upstairs.

"Hi Guy, what's happening?" A short, stocky man strode from behind the desk.

"Heavy stuff, you won't believe," Mark shook his hand vigorously.

"Try me," Sean grinned.

"Three days ago I was diving in Bimini, shooting some reef shots and I damned near drowned. How's that for starters?"

"You gotta be kiddin." Sean's mouth dropped open. "What happened?"

"Damn boat stranded me, scared the bejesus outta me."

"I guess." He paused, reassured himself that Mark was all right and said, "You gonna sue 'em?"

"Well, I was, but you know, I forgot all about it until just now." A look of wonderment passed over his face.

"I can see how you'd forget that . . . and your name."

"No, no, I'm serious. I've got something much more important to discuss than suing those idiots, although I should go after the morons." He scowled.

"What could be more important, other than celebrating your victory over their incompetence?" Sean interrupted.

"That's what's so great. This whole thing gave me a great idea you won't imagine. I've got an awesome concept for an emergency location device," he blurted out.

Amused by his young friend's enthusiasm, Sean folded his arms in front of him and eyed Mark curiously. "Okay, lets hear it."

Excitedly Mark outlined his plan.

Sean listened carefully. As the plan unfolded, he tapped his lips thoughtfully with his fingers, interrupting only twice to ask for technical elaboration.

"Well, what do you think?" Mark finished breathlessly.

Shaking his head slowly, Sean picked his words with care. "I think it has merit, but right now it's just one more idea written on a paper napkin as it were. And I've seen dozens of neat ideas scribbled on scrap paper or even neatly drafted on engineering paper. What do you want to do with it?"

"I want to get a more complete design down on paper and then patent the idea and manufacture the product. And I would like to involve you in the process, if you'd be interested."

"Hmmm." Sean eyed Mark keenly. "Certainly I'm flattered that you would ask me to get involved, but I think you're getting a little ahead of yourself." He put up one finger, "First, you better see about a patent." He extended another finger, "Second, you better figure out where the money's going to come from." He nodded toward Mark. "Until you come up with methods to jump those two hurdles, you may be just jerking off in the corner."

Sean saw Mark was hurt, but he could see no point in pretense. Obviously he hadn't the foggiest idea of what he was getting himself into.

"Look, I'm sorry." Sean leaned toward his friend and placed a hand on his arm, "but I've seen too many 'true believers' tilting at windmills, wasting their own and everyone else's time on projects that never reach fruition."

Mark looked down at his friend's hand, then withdrew his arm.

"Come on Mark. It really is a good idea, but — Tell you what." His voice softened. "You go ahead and see about a patent. I know a couple of people that just might be interested in a venture capital deal on a project like this."

Mark brightened noticeably.

"Now don't get excited," Sean cautioned, raising his hand. "You may have to talk to a hundred potential backers just to find one live one."

"I know. I've been warned—plenty," Mark grinned. "I already have an appointment with a patent attorney, so do what you can do."

"I do have one guy you should talk to. After you talk to your patent man, give me a call. I'll see if I can arrange a meet. The guy is ex-Navy, you may find him helpful. He's well connected."

"Great! Let's sign 'em up and get going!"

Sean groaned, "Another true believer, god help us all." But he smiled as he groaned, partially because he liked the concept and partially because he liked the way Mark was handling himself. Strange what nearly drowning can do to a man, he mused.

Mark hesitated, his expression thoughtful. "If someone asked you what are the three biggest problems in the world, what would you list?"

"Well, I don't want to hurt your feelings, but an emergency locator is not one of them." Sean laughed.

"I know. But seriously, what would you list?"

"A year or so ago I would have listed Communism, but only Cuba and a few Harvard professors take that seriously now, so I guess pollution would be number one, and global warming and maybe world hunger. Why?"

"Oh nothing. Yet. "Catch you later," Mark fired over his shoulder as he bounded down the stairs. He couldn't get downtown fast enough.

CHAPTER SIX
CONNECTIONS

Mark enjoyed the Ft. Lauderdale business district with its clean streets, unburdened by derelicts. Well, no derelicts, unless one counted the pigeons hanging around the courthouse looking for handouts. Even so, better than Miami, he could still speak English and be understood. He could even order a hamburger in English. Ordean Jacobs's office was located in a bank building, only one block away from the Federal Courthouse and the offending pigeons.

Not too shabby, Mark observed, as he parked in the garage. He walked slowly to the elevators, gathering his thoughts before talking to Jacobs. The massive building had an abundance of black glass highlighting the polished marble.

"Hello, may I help you?" The greeting floated in the air. The name plate on the desk defined the owner of the melodious voice as Jennifer Townes.

"Yes, Mark Hansen to see Ordean Jacobs," Mark projected in his best authoritarian tones.

"He'll be with you shortly," Jennifer smiled, "Just make yourself comfortable."

Could she see how nervous he was? No, decided Mark with relief. Long-haired well-built Jennifer was too busy being impressed with herself to take note of anyone else.

The reception area looked out over the new library building. To the left could be seen the new cultural arts center. As he gazed at the skyline Mark wondered how much of the county's new prosperity was financed with old cocaine dollars. Many successful businesses in Fort Lauderdale had been founded or expanded on the cash flows from the old grass and coke days, before the cocaine cowboys and the viciousness set in. Now they were legit. They paid their taxes, joined the chambers and climbed socially. Some even died peacefully in their sleep. He wondered if it mattered. Money laundering, drugs, pornography . . .

The solid oak furniture looked like something out of the Fountainhead from the 1930's. Black leather and dark woods; very masculine, with a remarkable absence of anything related to hi-tech or engineering.

"Do you enjoy Remington?" asked a voice from behind him.

"The statue on the desk or the gun?" Mark inquired, turning to confront a man in his early 60's, deeply tanned, white-haired and sporting a full white beard. Mark could picture him as the mayor of Tombstone.

"Either."

"Yes, actually, I like the statue."

"Good, you may stay."

"Mr. Jacobs, this is Mark Hansen," Jennifer made the introduction.

"Hello Mark, come on in. I'm just getting here myself."

Ordean Jacobs was robust and vigorous, with a ready smile and powerful handshake. Mark liked him immediately.

"Please sit down and be comfortable," the lawyer said, "may I have Jennifer bring you some coffee or a soft drink?"

Mark declined, but appreciated the grace of this man. "Mr. Jacobs," he started, "I've had no experience in patents, or in entrepreneurship for that matter, and I'd appreciate any guidance you could offer." One thing that Mark had learned from Fred was that there's no disgrace in ignorance; that could be cured. Only stupidity was terminal.

"I've been developing an idea that may need protection,"

he went on, "and I'd appreciate an explanation of what's involved in obtaining a patent, and what the costs would be."

Young and inexperienced, but bright, Jacobs sized him up. He readily understood why Fred liked this man. He was a lot like Billy, more than a surface resemblance.

"First let me explain a little about patents, and then if I can I will be happy to be of assistance." He pulled a pipe from his coat pocket and bit on it, but didn't light it. "To cut through all the legalese and get to the bottom line, a patent is simply a government permission that you may exclusively use your idea for 17 years and no one else is allowed to use it without your permission. That is oversimplified, but is the essence of it. The process takes from $5,000 to $15,000 in money and from 18 months to 36 months in time. This assumes the idea is patentable, and that it isn't unusually difficult or simple. It also assumes that the idea is worth protecting."

The attorney smiled kindly through the beard and pushed back in his chair. "Okay, so far?" He noted Mark's acknowledgment, and went on. "Here's a crash course in patents. The first thing, if you think you have an idea that is worth protecting, and by that I mean if you think it has commercial value – the first thing is to put it down in writing as completely as possible."

He pointed at Mark with the pipe stem, "In your case you should include rough sketches of any hardware, and so on, that's involved. Then I look over what you give me and, on the basis of my legal experience, I determine if it's worthwhile to do a patent search."

Mark was beginning to wish he could cut through all this junk, but he listened intently.

"That is, I make sure the idea is not so obvious as to be unpatentable, and that it's original and meets other legal requirements. If we agree that we should continue, then I will have a search made of patent records to see if the prior art, you know the previous patent files, already disclose or reveal your idea."

Mark started to interrupt but was glad he didn't.

"Almost always there will be some serious similarities in prior art to any idea. It's very rare to have a totally new idea. I then review the prior art and we discuss it. I will render a legal opinion as to whether or not I think we may obtain a patent." The pipe went back into its pocket.

"Remember, just because there's not already such a product on the market doesn't mean the idea is original or that a patent doesn't already exist. You'd be amazed at the number of ideas that are patented and never go to the market place."

Mark felt he'd be amazed if he absorbed half of what Ordean was throwing at him.

"If, after a business evaluation of the desirability of acquiring a patent, we decide to proceed with the application, then I'll have a patent artist prepare formal drawings and I'll write up what you claim to be the essence of your idea. Then we will submit the application." Mark thought that sounded good, until Ordean continued.

"Usually within six months we'll get a rejection on some technical grounds or on some other basis. That's when I really start to earn my money. We usually go back and forth with the Patent Office, and if all goes well, in about two years a patent will issue. I generally get a deposit to cover the cost of a patent search, and thereafter you'll be billed quarterly or however we work it out." Ordean paused, lifting his eyebrows and stroking his beard. "Any questions?"

Mark leaned forward. "Yes, Mr. Jacobs. Is it really necessary to file a patent application this early in the project?"

Ordean nodded approvingly at Mark. "Good question. Yes, it is desirable to file early. If someone else later comes up with the same or a similar idea, the timing of both the invention and the filing for protection of that invention may be critical. Second, you may forfeit your right to patent protection completely if you discuss or publish your idea or invention prior to protecting it legally. Once an idea is in the public domain, as we say, it cannot generally be protected."

"You mean if I just talk to people about the idea, it's published?" asked Mark incredulously.

"You can imagine the edges of this get a little fuzzy and it's much better to be safe than to find you have a successful product that you can't protect." Ordean paused. "But let's not get too far ahead of ourselves, and let's not get too involved with legal concerns. You have other matters that can better occupy your time. But you might find it interesting to know that two nearly identical products might each be patented individually if the claims made by the inventors were different and not mutually exclusive. That's why it's so important for the patent to be well drafted so no major loopholes are left for potential competitors."

Mark understood now why Fred insisted on this meeting with Ordean, and was grateful that he had.

"So, now tell me about your idea," Ordean urged.

Mark reviewed the entire concept, starting with the story of his harrowing experience and ending with a description of the airborne radar-reflector.

Ordean took notes and nodded. Occasionally he asked for clarification of a point, then lapsed back to silence, inviting Mark to continue. When Mark had finished, Ordean stroked his beard thoughtfully.

"There are already many types of radar reflectors in use on boats, and the idea of a locating balloon is not new. However, subject to a patent search, my initial impression is that you have a clean shot at a design patent at the least, and maybe even a utility patent. I would suggest that you write up your idea, give me some sketches and we'll do a patent search."

Mark felt encouraged. "How much should I write the check for?" he asked as he withdrew his checkbook.

"Save that for later," the lawyer told him, "I'll bill you and upon receipt of the patent search results, you may pay me." Ordean rose, extended his hand. "Good luck."

"Mr. Jacobs, if I had an idea for something, say in the field of pollution control or even radioactivity, would that be a lot more difficult or expensive?"

"Whole different ball game. Especially nuclear and particularly if the government gets involved. Why?" The lawyer silently re-appraised the young man. *Fred, my man, you just may have one hell of a protege or one hell of a loose cannon on the deck. Will he focus on one idea and carry it to completion?*

"Oh. Just wondering. Thanks for your help." Mark shook his hand firmly and left the office feeling almost as good as he had when he saw the Happy Camper coming toward him in the Bimini waters.

Jennifer validated his parking ticket with efficiency and a flirtatious glance. At one time Mark probably would have noticed and picked up on it. Not now.

When he called Sean, he was pleased to learn that a meeting was set with Tom Garret, a retired Navy officer. Tom, now a captain on a 185-foot yacht, suggested they meet at the hobby shop. "Since Tom is familiar with search and rescue and has himself stated that some type of improved emergency locating device is needed, I thought it natural for the two of you to get together." Mark agreed. "Also, Tom's financial connections might be very helpful to you," continued Sean. "Can you be at the store by 12:30 for lunch? His military connections sure wouldn't hurt, either, in marketing the product, if you're able to develop one."

Mark flinched at the "if" but remained quiet. He glanced at his watch. It was already close to noon. He jumped into the Explorer and streaked to the hobby shop.

Tom was already at the store when he arrived. "Let's roam on down to the Hitching Post for some chow and brews," Sean suggested.

Mark picked up the agenda. Social before business. Get better acquainted before deciding if they should dive into more serious conversation. He remembered a former talk with Sean. "It's all part of 'the waltz,' so you might just as well get used to it now. You're going to be doing 'the waltz' with a lot of prospective investors and god knows who else before you get this thing together. I did when I started the business, and everyone else I know has been through the same thing." When Mark frowned, Sean reassured him. "Don't worry, they can't kill you and they can't eat you, so relax and enjoy it."

The Post was a Western motif restaurant catering to locals and students. "Have you ever seen so many Rolexes on cowboys?" Tom commented after they were seated and put in their drink order – Sean, white wine, Mark, a Long Island Tea, and Tom, a JB and water.

"Mostly urban cowboys, and you oughtta see their houses," grinned Sean.

When the drinks arrived, they clicked glasses on the future. Mark sampled his drink and wished he'd ordered the wine instead. He hoped the drink wasn't indicative of how the meeting would go. Fortunately the outlook improved as the food arrived.

"Best damned Cajun tuna I've had in Florida," declared Tom.

Mark agreed, "The shrimp is excellent." Sean merely smiled over his salad. Seafood and salad in a Western restaurant—what the heck.

"You guys have to meet Walt, my buddy from Desert Storm. He has contacts all over the Pacific Rim." Sean had learned the quickest way to get Tom to open up was a war story or two. It worked . . .

"Remember when Republican Guard AAA bagged my chopper near As Salman and your lead platoon bailed me out?"

Sean grinned and shook his head, "Believe it or not, Mark, Tom and I didn't meet at that time. My special ops unit was attached to the 82nd Airborne. We supported the 18th Corps which was supposed to block the Iraqi retreat out of Kuwait."

"What the hell was a Navy chopper doing in the Desert?" Mark asked.

"It wasn't a Navy chopper. It was a Marine Huey. We were supposed to examine the damage to the As Salman airfields inflicted by cruise missiles." He paused sheepishly. "We were a little too low and a lot too slow, so we got nailed."

"It was years later that by chance we were talking, and pieced together his rescue by my guys. It was funny, because on paper neither unit was supposed to be there. Only someone who was actually on the ground would have known." Sean added.

Mark understood. His Army engineering unit went several places including As Salman and did several things with the 24th Infantry Division that never appeared in the official records.

Sean was right. No one understands the special bonding of combat veterans, who hasn't fired a shot in anger or been fired upon. Maybe it was like the gulf that separated women who'd given birth from those who hadn't — but more so. Before lunch was over they all knew what each other's 201's looked like, compared scars and agreed unanimously that war sucked.

"Damn, look at the time," Sean exclaimed, "We'd better get back to the shop. Barb'll wonder if we fell in." At the shop, the real discussion would begin.

Mark remembered his last phone conversation with Fred. "Stephens Law: In business, you don't get what you deserve, you get what you negotiate. So don't be too anxious. Make sure not to give up the farm too soon for too little. When you have a solid idea, make sure you get the full benefit of it." He'd seen engineers do just that, swapping a future for a bowl of porridge.

"Don't give away interest in the company in lieu of salary or expenses. Especially, don't give lawyers or accountants or brokers a piece of the action just to avoid some up front expenses. You're better off to scratch for the money, especially if the company stock becomes as valuable as you hope it will. Having said that, also don't get so greedy that you get stupid."

"Aren't I going to have to give up some of the company to raise the money I need to develop, build and market a product?" Mark had asked.

"Sure, it's better to have 60 percent of something, than 100 percent of nothing. But, don't let someone talk you out of big pieces of the company when their contribution may be minimal." Mark understood.

"So it's necessary to find some happy medium where I retain a reasonable percentage of the company, but make the deal attractive to an investor."

"Exactly. They want a better return on the investment than if they were to simply put money into CDs or blue chip stocks. The return must match the risk." In that last lecture, Mark started to see the larger picture.

Once settled around the conference table in Sean's office, Mark proceeded to recount his Bimini experience, explaining how it had stimulated his idea for an improved location device for divers or anyone else lost at sea.

Tom listened attentively. "You just joined a not very exclusive club of which I'm a charter member." Tom looked at Mark. "In the Gulf we went down in a Sea Hawk. Now with a battle group in that relatively small body of water, you'd think they would have found us in nothing flat. Five of us floated around in life jackets for nearly two days before they found us."

"Seriously small globe," agreed Mark. "You're right Tom, I've met several people who share our experience. It's so common there has to be a need there."

"Amen. I have a clipping file that has literally dozens of similar incidents documented. I've been accumulating them because I think they prove the need for an improved emergency location device." Tom stood up and paced as he expounded.

"My concept was some sort of round rubber inflatable balloon that could be automatically filled when submerged in water. For example, when a man fell overboard or when a pilot parachuted into the water. It would be a visual signal."

"That's neat," said Mark, "but a round balloon would blow down in windy weather. How about we make the balloon wing-shaped, instead?" He had Tom's full attention. "And how about a metalized film for the balloon material so the balloon would show up on radar? This way even small ship-borne search radars could find a survivor more than a mile away, and airborne radar probably more than 25 miles away."

Tom sat down. I'm glad Sean got us together, he thought. This kid has some smarts. Thank god he's no airheaded college kid, just pie in the sky with no practical application. "You know, for someone with no training in search and rescue you seem to have a good grip on the basic problems of finding survivors at sea," he praised Mark aloud.

"Thanks." Mark was genuinely grateful. He respected Tom and was glad to know it was mutual. "Look, we agree that there's a need for a product, and we even have some good idea of what it should be like." But it still isn't clear to me how to raise the money needed — or for that matter, exactly how much money to look for."

Tom responded directly. "I liked the ideas that you put foreword. I feel that some type of patent protection is needed, not only to prevent theft by potential competitors, but to make us more credible in the eyes of investors." He was cutting right through it. "I want to talk to some people who may be potential investors, but if I bring in the needed capital I will expect to be included as an equal partner in the business."

Mark flinched.

"Don't worry, I'm not looking for a free ride. I'd assume marketing responsibility, particularly with the government. And you, Mark, would assume operating responsibility."

Mark detected surprise in Sean's eyes. Caution was still the order of the day.

Tom continued, "My best guess, based on figures I developed for my version of the concept, would be that we need about a quarter million dollars." Sean's mouth opened slightly.

Mark tried to keep his best game face intact. "Your numbers may be a little low, based on some things I've been told, but I think you're in the ball park. How much equity do you feel we'll have to give up to raise that much?"

"Venture capital people will want 51 percent or more, but I think we should try to give up only 25 percent or 35 percent tops." He looked confident. After all, he knew the money people, and Mark didn't. "It might break out one-third for you, one-third for me and one-third for them—equal out. Of course, if they give up control they probably will still want a seat on the board of directors and they'll want their own corporate attorney to represent the company. Or they might not even be interested. We'll see."

Sean cautiously interjected. "Do you know who their attorney is?" Somehow he was sure Tom knew.

"Yes." Tom hesitated. "Ben Tinney, I think. Why?"

"Just wondered," Sean replied. He knew Tinney and didn't like him. But for now he kept silent. He glanced at Mark.

Mark wanted to talk to Sean, Fred and Ordean before accepting Tom's suggestions or making counter-proposals. Although he didn't want to give away too much, he had no immediate prospects for investors. He didn't want to be greedy and destroy a potential deal. Nevertheless, it was his idea and he didn't want to give away an equal share to someone else simply because he was bringing the money people to the table. Even so, he had a good feeling about Tom. He knew he had much to think about. He also knew there was still part of the success equation missing. He had the idea, Tom might help with the marketing, but they still needed technical skills that neither of them possessed.

"Let's do this, Tom," said Mark. "I'll pursue the patent, you talk to your people, and we'll get back together later in the week. Then maybe we can button down some numbers." He started to rise, then paused and settled again.

"One other thing Tom. While Sean and Paul might be of assistance in systems development, we need design and mechanical engineering help if we're going to develop a product that has market appeal as well as function."

"You don't know the half of it," declared Tom. Wait until you see the SOLAS requirements, the DOT regulations and the hoops the Coast Guard will put us through."

These were tests Mark hadn't been aware of. Tom's value seemed to increase by the minute.

Tom elaborated, "The Safety Of Life At Sea regulations, called SOLAS would apply to 33 countries, but in addition, there would probably be independent tests by other governments. Japan is very protectionist and might use testing to keep our product off their market until they could develop a knock-off."

"Glad you know that stuff, Tom. Tell you what, I'll concentrate on the mechanics and you watch out for the marketing." Tom nodded assent.

No formal agreement had been struck, but the natural flow was evident. Sean was pleased with himself. Well, guy, he praised himself, you "done good" putting those two together. It went together almost too easily. Sensing it was time for the meeting to wind down, Sean returned lightly to the military chat. "Mark, you two seem to have everything under control, but I would offer one piece of advice."

Mark looked expectantly from Tom to Sean.

"Yeah. Never get into a helicopter with Tom. Every time he goes up he either crashes in the desert or the ocean. Those Navy geeks can't keep anything in the air but their dicks."

"UP YOURS! You special ops types are nothing but SEAL wannabes," Tom fired back.

This is good, thought Mark, enjoying the laughter. Very good. He pushed away from the table. "Fellows, I have to pick up Linda. Tom, good meeting you. I'm looking forward to our next meeting." Tom's handshake was firm. Another good sign. "Sean, I'll call you later."

CHAPTER SEVEN
COMPLICATIONS

Linda was already waiting for him at Tugboat's. "So Mr. Genius, what's burning up those brain cells?" She pulled away from him, eyeing him at arm's length.

"Two interesting meetings, but I don't want to bore you to death. I know I've done nothing but talk about this locator thing lately, but I just can't seem to think of anything else, except you, of course."

Linda smiled encouragement. "I want to hear about the meetings."

From Mark's description of Ordean Jacobs, she felt good about him, even though she usually distrusted attorneys. She thought of the saying a Japanese student had told her: "If you would destroy an enemy, send him a Russian economist or an American lawyer." Hopefully Ordean was an exception.

About Tom, Linda wasn't so sure. For some reason she felt he might not be all that he seemed. She said nothing to Mark about these feelings because it was unfair to judge a person she hadn't even met.

"At any rate," continued Mark, "the crux of the problem is finding some technical help, in particular, a design engineer."

"Sugar, would you consider someone even if he, or she,

were young — and female?"

Mark pulled his drink closer, playing with the swizzle stick, and eyed Linda intently. He knew a loaded question when he heard one. "Let me put it this way. The person we hire may make or break the project, and with it, our financial futures. But with that as a given, I would consider anyone."

"You talked about the difficulty of finding someone you could trust who would work for a reasonable fee — yet who was competent. You know my friend Daphne Leland. She's just finishing her master's degree in mechanical engineering. Why not give her an interview?" Linda was doing her best soft sell. "You at least could have a meeting and then draw your own conclusions."

Two days later Daphne drove up from the engineering campus at the U of Miami and met Mark and Linda at the apartment. The three met beside the swimming pool. Usually deserted in the early morning hours, it was a good place to combine fun and business.

At once Mark felt good about Linda's friend. She was warm, put on no airs and obviously knew where she was going. Mark presented his idea, elaborating on the problems they were facing, and Daphne immediately categorized them.

"If I understand you correctly," Daphne reiterated, "you need help in three areas—design, high pressure gases, and balloon technology. I'd be interested in talking further about the project with you and your associates. Based on what you've told me, I know I can make a contribution." Her assurance pleasantly surprised both Linda and Mark.

"You realize I don't have the final say-so. But I'll arrange a meeting for us with Tom and Sean, maybe Monday, if that's convenient, and we'll see where it goes from there." It was suitably non-committal.

Daphne understood completely. "As far as I know, Monday would be good for me, if it's convenient for everyone else. If you'll just let me know after you discuss it with your friends."

"Works for me." Mark nodded agreement.

"If you two are finished with business, why don't we take

a dip in the pool?" Linda offered.

"Sounds tempting, but I really need to get back to the Gables," Daphne replied. She rose and approached Mark. "Mark, it was great meeting you." She extended her hand.

"Daphne, we'll be in touch." He formally shook her hand. He found his eyes following her as she walked from the pool to her car. She was much more than he had expected.

On the drive back to the campus, Daphne reviewed the meeting with Mark. Yes, he was nice. Yes, she liked him. Yes, she thought she could work with him. Yes, he was very nice, she repeated. Linda was lucky. She was happy for her friend. Mark would make a great husband. Peter's face flashed before her. "I wish I could treat you the way I should," she said aloud.

"Why don't I drive Daphne up to Davie on Monday?" Linda suggested to Mark after Daphne had left. "Everyone could meet at the hobby shop. I could get together with Barbara, while you, Daphne, and whoever conduct business. It'll make things easier on Daphne who doesn't know the area. She could use the company on the trip up and back, and you guys could talk everything over after we leave."

"O.K., hon, if you wish," Mark replied absently.

Although she did not verbalize it, Linda was very comfortable with Daphne, but was also aware of how attractive her friend was. She trusted her and Mark, she just felt better being in the vicinity. After all, Daphne was several inches taller, slightly slimmer and had marvelous muscle tone.

"Hon, let's go on up and relax a little." Mark bounded from the pool in one powerful motion.

" . . . and relax?" she teased, swimming toward the ladder.

"Whatever." He grinned as he assisted her from the pool.

They paused in the tiled entryway to the apartment. "Do you need any help getting out of that suit?" He playfully leered.

"Sure. Do you have any paint remover on you?" She joked back. She was confident of her appearance, as she and Daphne swam almost daily to keep in shape.

She walked toward the bedroom, then stopped. Mark

watched as she undid her halter-top. She grinned over her shoulder, "Eat your heart out."

He observed that other than height the distinguishing difference between the girls was their hair. Daphne wore her hair short as a concession to the practicalities of working around machinery. Linda's flowed over her shoulders. She was striking, framed against the backdrop of the bay, he thought.

He skinned off his swim suit, looked directly into her eyes, and said, "You too."

They raced for the bed. It was a tie.

On Monday, Mark was getting ready for the meeting in Davie. "Tell me a little more about Daphne." He wanted to be well prepared for the meeting.

"I think her dad owned a foreign car repair business. She was the eldest child." Linda strained to remember anything useful, but not betray any confidences. "She liked to play with tools. Her brothers teased her until her dad pointed out she was better on a lathe and milling machine than they were."

"Her biggest problem now is not injuring the pride of her male classmates." Linda smothered a laugh. "It's tough on a girl when she has to fix her date's sports car or whatever, and still look feminine." Maybe some secrets are best kept, even from fiancées, she mused.

As the girls walked into the hobby shop, Linda was glad she'd taken extra care in dressing that day. It wasn't that she was jealous of Daphne, but it was reassuring that the admiring looks the two of them drew as they walked over to the service counter were at least equally divided. Barbara was at the counter and greeted Linda.

Linda was looking forward to a chat. They had much in common, including a love of deep-sea fishing.

"Guess what?" Barbara anticipated her. " I just got a video tape of marlin and sail fishing in Costa Rica." They were set for the afternoon. Barbara buzzed the intercom in Sean's office, then sent Daphne upstairs to the meeting.

"Daphne Leland, I'd like you to meet Tom Garret and

Sean Knight. Sean walked up to Daphne and hugged her in greeting.

"Let's dump these vultures and go for a ride." Gracefully he released her, leaving her bemused.

Mark envied the natural way Sean handled himself with women. It didn't matter, young or old, timid or bold, Sean seemed to always do and say just the right thing.

Tom extended his hand formally, obviously annoyed that he was going to have to deal with someone who looked like a novice. *Lord save us from well intentioned, unqualified skirts. I had to put up with affirmative action in the Navy, but not here. And she's a college kid on top of it . . . Jesus . . . Why do they insist on going for jobs they're unqualified for?*

Sean caught Tom's attitude in his body language and wondered if Mark had also. He saw that Daphne had got it. *That's fine with me, I've won over tougher men than he,* she thought angrily. *For all I care he can take his Navy macho bullshit and blow it out his tail pipe.* She'd already learned that beauty could be one of a female's greatest handicaps in the professional world.

Mark leaned back against the wall. He had some misgivings about the level of Daphne's experience, but no doubts at all about her competence. He watched Tom, trying to get a sense of where he was coming from.

"To get things started, let me just briefly describe the invention and what we suspect are the likely problems." Mark outlined the design concept while Tom, Daphne and Sean listened.

When Mark finished he turned toward the Texan. "Tom, do you have anything to add?"

A lot! thought Tom to himself, his eyes tightening. We'll straighten this bitch out in a heartbeat. He forced a smile. Direct attacks were out. Instead, he began by asking Daphne, "What engineering experience have you had?"

"I worked with an aerospace company doing engineering design work after graduating from R.P.I. I left that job to come to Miami for my Masters. During undergraduate school I co-oped at NRL, you know, Naval Research Laboratories in D.C."

Damn. Well let's see what you're made of, young lady. "Do you think you have enough experience to design and develop the product that is weatherproof, floatable and durable in addition to meeting the other design requirements?" Tom proceeded to expand on the design requirements.

As he talked he felt he was making progress. With each requirement for product performance, Daphne seemed to get a little more agitated.

By the time he'd fully explained what he expected from the product and from the production facility, Daphne was almost openly aghast. My god, she reflected. They really don't have a clue how difficult a task they've set! The chauvinism she could handle; the technical naivete was a shock.

Tom appraised his victim smugly. "Gotcha." he thought to himself.

Sean had been studying Daphne intently during Tom's talk, and now he felt it was time. He was almost certain he was reading her, but wanted to be sure. "Is it my imagination, or are you uncomfortable with either the people or the project?" He caught a faint smile at the corner of Daphne's mouth. Encouraged, he continued, "I get that impression, but you're not saying anything. So, what's the deal?"

Daphne summoned up all the tact and determination she could muster and said, "Apparently no one else in the room has the foggiest idea of how difficult a project you're embarking on. Your parameters are not totally practical. I have the impression you don't have realistic expectations of the lifting ability of helium, nor a complete comprehension of the difficulty of containing it. Furthermore, you may not have a realistic view of how compact we could make the product. Based on what I've heard, you have an unrealizable target price for selling the product."

Mark and Tom were stunned. When they regained their composure, it was Tom who spoke first. Although he was visibly irritated he came short of being insulting.

"Young lady, by your own admission, you don't have all that much practical experience. You have none in search and rescue, nor have you undergone the survival experiences that Mark and I have had. I can't help wondering why you're so depreciating toward the project, and why you made such harsh judgements."

Tossing her head, Daphne rose from her seat and started pacing the room. "You're right to some extent about practical experience, but let me point out a few facts. Helium can only lift four ounces per cubic foot of volume. You want to put three cubic feet of helium in only three cubic inches of pressure vessel, which means you would have a working pressure over 15,000 psi." She hesitated, letting the first blow sink in.

"Even if we could find a way of safely filling the vessel at that pressure, the cost of making such a vessel would drive the market price of the product to the moon." She was jabbing at obvious weak points.

"Not only that, but if we found a way of doing the pressure vessel, a control valve alone would probably cost about half the price you wanted to charge at retail for the product. So how would we provide markup to the distributors and dealers, much less any operating profit?" The right cross.

"Even if you could solve those problems, there remains the problem of finding a material that would reflect radar, hold helium, be very light and still be durable enough to be practical in a survival situation, and still be cost effective." The left upper cut.

"In other words, if you keep the design parameters you would price yourselves out of the market. But if you would revise your design parameters, it might, just might be possible to achieve a cost effective product that would be useable in a survival situation." The knock down.

"It is my suggestion that you completely rethink the project before going any further." Gracefully she settled into a chair. Go to a neutral corner.

Tom and Mark did their best to remain civil and polite but they were clearly wounded. Maybe she should have been gentler, Daphne reflected. Tom's chauvinism really got to her. Their technical naivete had caught her by surprise.

Sean was impressed. Although somewhat taken aback by the virulence of Daphne's attack, he recognized that her analysis was not only astute, but appeared to be backed by facts, which she seemed to have at her fingertips. "Golly, maybe we should have gone for that ride," he drawled, interrupting what looked like a bloody second round. "Why don't you tell us poor saddle tramps why you're so sure?" Even Tom had to laugh at Sean's terrible imitation of John Wayne.

Picking up on Sean's lead, Daphne came back, "I didn't intend to rile anyone, but I think it important not to walk into a bunch of cow pies when you know they're there." Sean's ready smile confirmed she was on the right track. "Due to contractual agreements I cannot tell you the nature of my consulting work with the aerospace company, but it did include government contract work with high pressure gasses." Wave to the crowd.

She could not tell them her work was on radar reflecting decoys that were nothing more than radar-reflecting balloons with specially designed reflection characteristics. They could not possibly find a more able person for the project, but she couldn't tell them why.

She continued, "With my training and background plus the high pressure work I've done, I certainly can handle the helium supply part of your engineering problems." Offer your hand to your adversary after the knock down.

"I feel that since the balloon is new to everyone, I am as likely as anyone to be able to solve that also." Exit the ring gracefully.

If it were up to me, Sean thought to himself, I'd hire her in a heartbeat. He said nothing.

Mark felt that Daphne had done an adequate job of explaining why she felt she could do the job, and she'd asked for the opportunity. Now came the tough part. Did she really know what she was talking about. Were their expectations wrong? Should she be hired? She had really hit them between the eyes about redesigning the concept, and he didn't know at this point what to do. And not the least, could she get along with Tom, or vice versa?

"Daphne, we appreciate you taking the time to come up and talk to us about the project. We'll let you know as soon as we reach a decision about what we're going to do next."

Technical K.O.?

Daphne realized she had taken a chance challenging their assumptions, but she felt it had been her best shot at the project. It was now a matter of personalities, not competence. She knew in her heart she was right for the project. But were they smart enough to admit it?

She also reminded herself on the subject of knowing one's heart that she must be careful in her relationship with Mark. A shame he was Linda's fiancée and her potential employer. She heard her father's admonition, "You do not foul your own nest, missy." Distance, she warned herself.

CHAPTER EIGHT
CONFLICT

Dammit, he should never have allowed Tom to talk him out of hiring Daphne. Mark sat at his desk staring glumly at a blue print. "Trust me, August Vasilefski is experienced and mature," Tom had assured him.

Mark fumed, mentally flailing himself, "If I cannot run this project well, how could I hope to interest anyone in a really big project?" Well Tom was half right, August was so mature, he was spoiled rotten. We're weeks behind schedule on the machine to weld and fill the helium cylinders. Mark bashed himself for yielding. The delay infuriated him. It forced a confrontation he'd hoped to avoid. Taking a deep breath, he pushed away from his desk and strode toward Tom's office. Maybe if he did this on Tom's home turf he'd take it a little better.

"Goodaye Mate," he started lightheartedly.

"Looking troubled, Mark." Noting the expression on Mark's face, Tom rose deliberately from his chair. "What's the problem?" He rested on the desk's edge.

"Tom if we go any slower we'll be going backwards."

"Well, these quarrels between you and Augie about machine design aren't helping. Don't you think one of you'd better decide which of you is going to engineer the plant?" Tom snapped.

Undeterred, Mark leaned against the wall, lowered his

eyes and continued, "Look I thought we agreed that you would be responsible for marketing and I would be responsible for operations. Augie was supposed to engineer the plant. He is not getting it done. We should not have hired him."

"Mark I can't sell something that doesn't exist," Tom snarled. "So I thought I'd help get things going. Augie has a good track record and I can't see why you two can't get along. I'm getting the feeling that too many cooks are spoiling the broth."

"Are you trying to say it's my fault because the guy you brought on board can't cut it?"

Tom was literally chewing his tongue. Mark was right about Augie; he wasn't pulling his own weight. About the arguments . . . he wasn't so sure.

"All right Mark. You are responsible for administration, and you bear ultimate responsibility for the success or failure of the plant. So maybe you'd better get on the ball and get us a plant and a product." His was the smile of a horned rattlesnake. He arched forward, waiting.

Mark knew where the buck stopped.

"Very well," Squaring his shoulders he triggered the intercom, "Joyce, please ask August to meet Tom and me in Tom's office."

The older man soon ambled into the office, unperturbed. Mark directed Augie toward a chair and gazed piercingly at the engineer. "Augie, I am concerned about using Lexan to construct the retaining assembly on the weld-fill machine." Augie squirmed uncomfortably in the chair.

"I realize I'm not a trained mechanical engineer," he nodded at Tom, "but I've studied enough materials science to know it's foolhardy to build the assembly that way." The engineer glanced first at Tom, then briefly at Mark. His face flushed and his neck reddened. Forked veins stood out on his bald head.

Subtle as a recoilless rifle, thought Tom angrily. His eyes rolled back and he shook his head.

Augie bristled, "You're paying me to do the engineering. Do you want me to do my job or not?" He looked at both men. In Tom's eyes he saw support. Mark was delivering cold distrust.

Clearly he'd lost faith. Augie winced.

Mark turned to Tom, his eyes flashing, "Does this make sense to you?" Leaning back on the desk, Tom was silent for a moment.

"Look Mark, you just told me to butt out of the engineering. Why don't you make up your own mind and either let Augie do his job or replace him?" Tom drawled, smiling broadly and comfortably as he rose from the desk.

"All right, do it your way, Augie. But you damn well better be right!" Mark's flinty eyes and flared nostrils chilled Augie to the core.

"It'll be okay. You'll see," Augie reassured his boss after Mark had left.

"I know. I know," Tom reassured him as he escorted Augie from the office. Returning, he slammed the door. Rounding the desk he kicked the wastebasket across the floor. "Son-of-a-bitch."

"God help us." Mark muttered angrily. What was wrong with Tom that he couldn't see the stupidity of using plastic in a high pressure, high temperature, high electric flow environment? He resolved to keep a close watch on the progress of the assembly and its testing.

"It's safe," Augie yelled.

"Safe, my ass." Paul's massive finger waved beneath the older man's nose. "They hadn't even invented Lexan when you were in school, you stupid wonk."

"Come on Paul, that's a little harsh," Tom interrupted from a safe distance. He saw Paul's biceps bulging as he shook his hand in Augie's face.

"Fellows, it's not a case of textbook knowledge. No one knows what this is going to do and I suggest you look for the safest method." Sean spoke so softly the others grew quiet in an effort to hear him.

"Be that as it may. It's my job and I don't recall asking your opinions." Augie turned on the helium pump. "I'll prove that it works." He opened the valve.

"Whoosh . . . whomph, whooosh . . . whomph," The pump cranked up, the pressure gauge jumped.

"I'd stand back if I were you." Paul nudged Sean away from the machine. "I figure it's . . ."

"BRAMMMMMMMMNNNNN . . ." Plastic flashed past their faces.

"Plinnkkkk . . . clatter . . .clunckle . . ." Debris flew in all directions. Chalk-white, Tom teetered back from the blast. "Son-of-bitch," he muttered. His arm stung. Small pieces of plastic peered out from the flesh, gradually turning red as trickles of blood appeared. "You bastard," he yelled at Augie.

Mark was talking to Fred on the phone when his conversation was interrupted by a sudden loud bang that echoed through the rear corner area of the plant. "God-dammit, I knew it!" Mark threw the phone aside as he ran toward the door.

"Be careful, Joyce," Mark cautioned as he raced past his secretary into the production area. It was best that he had not witnessed the prelude to the explosion. The aftermath was grim enough. Mark entered the plant and was confronted with plastic debris imbedded in the entrance door. Near the weld-fill machine he glimpsed Sean, Paul, Augie and Tom. The machine lay shattered.

He scanned for damage. The men appeared uninjured at first glance. Pieces of metal were twisted and thrown about. A ruptured helium pipe approximated where the mechanism had once operated. A quick look at the gauges showed that an entire K cylinder of helium had dumped. Dust was settling and joining scraps of plastic and metal on the floor.

Eyes bulging, neck distended, Paul stalked over to August. "You degenerate son of a bitch, who told you that you're an engineer? I doubt you can even spell engineer. Do you realize your stupid ass just about got us killed?"

"Easy Paul." Sean rushed toward Augie, trying to get in between Paul and his probable target. With relief he saw Augie shrug, look a little dejected, and then just calmly turn and walk toward the door.

"You sleazy weasel, come back and take it like a man."

Paul raged. Saliva spewed as he yelled. White eyeballs turned red as blood pumped furiously. "Wimp!"

"You guys okay?" Mark appeared. "What happened? Any injuries?" His heart pounded. Sweat soaked his shirt.

"Chamber blowout, just like you said," Sean muttered, shaking his head in disgust.

"What was the chamber pressure?" he yelled to Sean.

"Only 4500 pounds per square inch."

"Thank God. Imagine if the booster pump engaged and the pressure was 9,500!" Abruptly he scanned the warehouse. Mark raced toward the front door where Augie was just exiting.

Tom followed, blood freely flowing down his arm. "Shit happens. No way I'm going to apologize to Mark," he muttered as he ran toward the lobby.

Sean, in pursuit of Tom, stopped suddenly upon entering the lobby. Mark had overtaken Augie and was standing between him and the front door. The veins stood out in Mark's neck. Small beads of sweat were on his forehead and on his upper lip. "You're FIRED," he barked, "We will mail anything we owe you. Don't ever come in that front door again."

Augie started to open his mouth. He looked into Mark's eyes and quickly wished he hadn't. What he saw there made his bowels move. Mouth clamped shut, shoulders slouched, the engineer slunk out the door. He kicked a pebble on the driveway. "Aw crap, it's a dumb idea anyway."

Sean was laughing. "That wasn't exactly textbook management technique, but even Ken Blanchard would give you an A plus on the one minute reprimand!"

Without even acknowledging Tom's presence, Mark picked up the lobby telephone and dialed Daphne's number. "Daphne, this is Mark Hansen. I find I have an opening on my engineering staff and if you're still interested, I'd like to employ you." Ptooey, the taste of humble pie rankled.

"Why don't I come up tomorrow morning and we can discuss this?" Daphne was noncommittal. Mark didn't blame her. They needed her to finish the project and that was all he cared about at the moment.

Promptly at nine a.m., Daphne pulled up in front of the plant in a red Chrysler Le Baron convertible. "Bing . . . Bong." The entrance security bell sounded.

"A little paranoid, aren't we?" she teased Mark.

Both Tom and Mark were slightly overboard on security, but Daphne actually liked that, since she too would be safe in the building. She expected they would be putting in some long hours.

To Mark's relief, there was no sign of malice or vindictiveness in Daphne's manner.

"Mark, Tom how are you? Why don't you brief me on where the project stands? After that, you can fill me in on what would be expected of me, and we can talk compensation." Mark figured the price of playing poker had just gone up, big time.

As he followed her into the plant, he observed that she looked very attractive in her blue cotton jump suit. Although selected to be functional, it left no doubt as to the gender of the person neatly encased by it. He walked Daphne to the rear of the building and showed her the balloon machine and cylinder welder as well as the remains of the weld-fill machine.

Even though Linda had told him Daphne was a first-rate mechanic and he was aware of her formal mechanical training, he wasn't ready for Daphne's response to the condition of the plant. Taking a long hard look at the weld-fill machine, she sighed, shook her head and turned calmly to Mark. "We're up to our ass in alligators aren't we?" she grinned. Mark stifled an embarrassed laugh.

"Where the hell did you guys find that clown?" She struck the tool chest with a wrench.

Mark blinked. He started to speak.

She sucked in her breath and caught herself. "Oh I'm sorry. I know that sounded incredibly bitchy and I promised myself I'd behave." She averted her eyes. "Of course you already know he could have killed himself or you or Tom or one of the employees."

Mark's eyes tightened. He placed a conciliatory hand on her arm. She met his gaze directly. "Daphne, let's clear the air. You were never second best in my mind, but it's my fault. I should have never given in to political pressure." He nodded at Tom.

"It wasn't fair to the company and it wasn't fair to Augie." He paused, assuring himself of her attention. "I had serious doubts about his ability to do the job. It's not right to get mad at a turtle when it can't fly like an eagle. Still, it was my final decision and I accept full responsibility for it."

Daphne nodded, her eyes softening. "Don't beat yourself up. This is cutting-edge technology and you're new at it."

"You're right, but that is no excuse. Bottom line, I very much need your help and I want you to work with me. But if this is going to be a problem, let's face it right now."

"Apology accepted. We have no problem. You keep on saying what's on your mind like you just did, and we're not going to have any problems." She tilted her head and eyed him provocatively. "But thanks for sharing that with me."

What she had not said was that she noticed his use of "work with" instead of "work for." Whoever had called Mark immature had wronged him terribly.

With no further preliminaries, Daphne strolled over to the tool chest and wheeled it over to the weld-fill machine. She looked directly at Tom and Mark. "If you'll excuse me," she said, then promptly disappeared under the machine.

Mark grinned at Tom, "I think we've just been given permission to go back to doing whatever it is we do." As they headed back toward their offices Mark continued, "The other day Sean was saying you served on nuclear boats."

"About half the time I was in. Why?"

"No special reason. I just wondered how you felt about them."

"Quiet, clean, fast, deadly."

"Clean?"

"Compared to diesel-electric sure."

"What about . . ."

"Never gave it a thought. It was just there."

"Ummmm." Mark continued to his office.

Tom stood watching, puzzled.

CHAPTER NINE
QUEEN OF DARTS

Two hours passed. Mark suggested to his secretary, "Joyce, you might want to go back and see if Daphne needs anything. Brief her on where the ladies rooms are and anything else you feel important from a practical viewpoint."

Minutes later his secretary returned. "Wow!" she exclaimed.

Mark looked up. "What happened? Did you hear a racy story?"

Grinning broadly, Joyce shook her head. "You know, I never said anything about Augie and I try to mind my business, but the new engineer really has things sized up already."

Mark looked puzzled. "What did she say?"

"Oh it's not what she said to me," Joyce said. " I went out as you suggested, and I guess I was too quiet because I heard her talking. When I got closer I realized she was talking to herself, but out loud, you understand."

"So, what did she say?"

". . . Well, the conversation was sort of like this: ' . . . dumb shit, son-of-a-bitch, incompetent asshole,' and then it got rougher so I made some noise and let her know I was there. I told her I shared her views."

"I don't know if she knows a spanner from a spittoon but

she sure has the right attitude hasn't she?" Joyce summed up.

"I guess she'll take some getting used to, but yes, I think she has the right attitude and I do have a lot of confidence in her. I like the way she jumped in and tackled the toughest job in the plant first." Mark understood it was not good management policy to discuss one employee with another, but he saw nothing wrong with sharing compliments.

To himself he prayed, Let's hope I'm right this time. I can't afford any more screw-ups. For the first time in many weeks Mark felt good about the company. The future looked favorable again, and it was none too soon. They were in trouble.

At lunch Tom had reinforced the feeling. "My investors are concerned about our being over budget. They're getting antsy."

"Frankly, Tom, I don't blame them. I can imagine how you must feel since your connections brought the money into the company. Your butt, just like mine, is on the line with the investors. It's a damn shame too, because I have another idea in mind."

"Don't you think we better get this puppy up and running before you waste any time and energy on another project?"

Tom knew it was more than just their butts that were on the line. As they missed objectives and schedules had slipped, the pressure had mounted. He was feeling it.

"Point well taken," Mark admitted sheepishly. Late in the afternoon, a dirty disheveled Daphne walked into Mark's office. She said curtly, "I think you'd better get Tom in here." Wearily she settled onto a chair beside the desk.

Mark buzzed Tom on the intercom. "Hey, guy, if you don't have someone with you, how about joining a pow-wow with Daphne and me in my office?"

Tom strolled in and took a seat.

Daphne was resolute. She looked from Tom to Mark, then back again, and finally said, "I can give you the straight scoop or I can sugar coat it. But just remember, we're not in Greece and we don't shoot the bearer of the message."

Tom flashed his ingratiating West Texas smile and Mark simply nodded for her to continue.

"I don't need to tell you we have major problems here.

My best guess is that we're looking at around $350,000 to finish the production facility—turn key. That assumes you'll use a die cutting press to cut out the balloons. That is strictly to get the plant up and running, not counting the inventory cost or marketing expense or such." She waited for a reaction to the grenade she'd just tossed.

Mark did some quick arithmetic in his head. "She's close, I make it more like a half a million to have a decent shot at getting to the marketplace. That assumes no more major catastrophic setbacks and that the employees could stay with a reasonable learning curve."

Tom scrutinized Mark and Daphne. "As you know, our materials and labor costs will be much higher during the first month or so, as employees are trained and systems debugged. If I were looking for money I'd ask for twice what my calculations said I needed, just to be safe. That doesn't come from a book, it just comes from 30 years of hard knocks.

Daphne turned toward him, chin high. "I know that I may sound a little bit textbook-ish, and I am. My figures come right out of the computer. But I take no offense at your idea of doubling the number. If you're going to screw up, best be on the side of caution. My dad told me you never want to have to go back to an investor once you've told them how much you need. So I'm comfortable with the higher number." A slight bow toward Tom summed up her comments.

"So what you two are saying is that I should figure on a million to get the job done?" Mark knew what the marketing plan called for, what the sales terms would be. They could move the goods quickly and collect just as quickly, to avoid crushing cash flow problems.

Mark pushed back into his chair and looked at Daphne, then at Tom. "Let me see if I understand. I blundered in selecting an engineer, so we pissed away the best part of a quarter million dollars and months of time. Now we need a full million to save our fannies. Naturally that assumes no one else gets to the market in the meantime or that some other major catastrophe doesn't befall us. Is that about all?"

"You've got it." Daphne leaned back, pressed her lips together and waited.

Mark and Tom fell silent. This was the worst emotional roller coaster Mark could imagine. He'd gone from near death in the Islands, to the heights of joy with Linda. He'd flown high with the excitement of creating a design and obtaining a patent, raising the money to get the company started; then plunged to the depths, as engineering failure after failure made it appear the project would never get off the ground, either figuratively or literally.

Tom broke the silence."If I were immature, I'd let this situation drive me straight to the nearest bar."

Mark shoved his note pad aside. "If I were immature I would let this situation drive me straight to the nearest bar."

Daphne laughed and stood up. "I guess I may be immature because I'm going to let this situation drive me to the nearest bar. Where is it?"

"Follow me," grinned Tom.

Mark and Daphne jumped into their cars and trailed Tom several blocks down Powerline to a freestanding building.

As they got out of their cars, Tom winked at Mark. To Daphne he said, "You go on in and we'll be right there, I just need to ask Mark something." They walked up to the door and opened it for her. Daphne walked carefully through two swinging doors. A long wooden bar was to her right and behind the bar was a tall redheaded barmaid, nude. Daphne turned left to leave and saw an elevated stage surrounded by men in seats watching three nude girls dancing. A large bearded figure rose from a chair and reached up to stuff money in the garter of the dancer nearest him. The dancer shifted position to give her benefactor a better view.

Daphne banged back through the swinging doors. Mark and Tom were pretending to be discussing business as they waited beside the door.

"I'd prefer a bar where the guys are performing next time." She smiled demurely as she headed toward her car.

"Okay. Bad joke. Come on, the real bar is at the other end

of the building. We'll even buy," choked Tom between laughs.

"Just remember, paybacks are hell," Daphne chuckled. She'd been to strip joints with the mechanics from her Dad's garage, but she wasn't going to spoil the boys' fun by letting on.

The bar turned out to be a country western place that catered mostly to construction workers. God, I don't believe this place, thought Daphne. I've never seen so many red-necks in one place. Well I'm dressed down just right. She smiled wryly, viewing her disrepair in a mirrored window.

Daphne might have felt out of place, but Tom was right at home. Dance floor—live band—dartboard—Hank Jr. on the wall. What more could one ask?

"Been in plenty of these during my tours," he remarked as he headed toward the bar.

"Been in one or two myself," Mark said, not to be outdone. Mark liked certain country singers, particularly Reba and Garth. Linda preferred Willie and Whalen and the rest. Mark missed her.

"I'll bet," Daphne interjected sarcastically, as she spotted a dartboard. Thank God, one sign of civilization. She'd spent many hours in an English pub near her dad's garage.

"I can see that Mr. Tom is lost in the music," Daphne said to Mark. "So let's throw some darts."

"You two get in line while I call home and let Momma know where I am." "Momma" was his wife, Mona. Ordinarily, Tom wouldn't have extended this courtesy but he knew hard times were coming and he wanted to do his best to smooth the waters before the storm overtook them.

"Save us a place while I call Linda." Mark followed Tom to the phones.

"Hi sugar, Tom and Daphne and I are at the Country Cattle Call or something like that." He described the place. "Just wanted to let you know I'm thinking about you and I wondered if you'd like to come on up and join us?"

"Honey, I'd love to, but it's such a drive and I'm buried with homework. I'll see you later this evening, won't I?"

"You better know it."

"Tell me all about it later."

The tone of her voice made him wish it were already later.

"See you soon, sugar."

As she replaced the phone she smiled. It was nice of Mark to be considerate and call.

"Next up?" One of the team at the board asked the room.

"Right here. What'ch'a playin?" Tom chimed in.

"Two Daniels."

"How do ya play?" Tom loved new games.

"Simple. We have six shot glasses filled with Jack Daniels. Each numbered, each bigger than the one before it. You throw a dart. Any number from one to five, you drink the shot number you throw. Anything over five, you drink the big shot glass."

"Makes sense to me, but why call it Two Daniels?" Mark asked, knowing he shouldn't.

"Well you're supposed to listen to Charlie Daniels while you play, pardner." The answer came from a big Georgian that everyone called Tex. It figured.

Everyone snickered. "Seriously, after a few rounds you need to dance off some of the dart game, y'know." Tex finished.

"I knew I shouldn't have asked," he muttered to Daphne.

"If it's okay with you, let's play teams," Daphne suggested.

"Sure, we got let's see, six people, let's make it three teams of two each. How about a little side bet on who'll be the winners after three rounds of tosses?" Tex asked. They agreed.

"You," Tex pointed to Tom," and me will stand the filly and the dude, and Ace and Slick here," He picked up the darts.

Mark wasn't sure he liked being called a dude, and he was sure he didn't like Daphne being called a filly, but in Rome . . . Besides, he liked the team assignments.

Daphne reminded herself not to throw too well. She knew male egos were easily bruised in any game of skill. On the other hand it was going to be a long drive home. She didn't want to throw down too many big shooters.

While Daphne walked a delicate tight rope, Tom and Mark tried to out-macho each other and the other dart throwers.

"Nice throw." Tex slapped Tom on the shoulder.

Mark tossed a seven.

"Bad throw Bozo."

Mark spun around to face the wise acre.

"Bad throw Bozo."

Mark was facing a huge green parrot now arrogantly perched on Slick's shoulder.

"Bad throw, Bozo."

Deciding it was impossible to out talk a parrot, he silently sought out a bar stool. Slick politely withheld comment as the bird alternately preened his feathers and glared at the dart throwers.

"Better luck next time, dude" To Mark — from Tex.

Mark's concentration wasn't a hundred percent on the game, so he wound up drinking more than his share of large glasses of Jack Daniels.

"Too bad they don't have Long Island Iced Tea," he thought glumly, but his spirits were lifted as the two Daniels, Jack and Charlie started to work upon him.

At the end of the third round of tosses, Mark's dart prematurely slipped away from his grip as he threw. He was astonished to see the dart land on number two, his best toss of the evening.

"Now it comes out. The dude has been sandbagging us," Daphne and Tom laughingly accused. Mark wisely refrained from commenting.

Following the good example of the group before them, Mark suggested, "Let's dance off some of the booze before we drive home." Daphne agreed.

"Sorry folks, but I gotta split," Tom had gained some wisdom in his years. Mona was expecting him. He knew this was no time for Texas macho bullshit to get him into difficulty at home.

"Nice dart game, ma'am." He leaned toward Daphne and winked knowingly. He shook Mark's hand and departed.

"Know how to Texas Two Step?" the dude asked the filly.

"Not'chet, but I'm a hankerin to larn," she replied.

Quickly she picked up three country dances including the Cotton Eye Joe. The live band started to intermingle some slow dances, mostly crossover pops.

"This is disgusting, I actually like this crappy music," Daphne grinned. The western swing was fun to dance to. To her amazement she discovered she was having a good time. But she was a little disquieted as she realized she and Mark were on their third slow dance together. She was dancing closer to him than she felt she ought to be. Moist palms and the way he moved with her told her that Mark was also thinking of things other than business.

"What?" He edged away slightly, looking down at her.

Color rose in Daphne's cheeks. How could he know what she was thinking?

"What what?" She teased.

"You just got a sort of . . . different look on your face, like . . ." He shook his head slowly.

"That clock can't be right," Daphne exclaimed self-consciously.

"Damn. It is." Their eyes met. Slowly he eased further away from her. "We better git a go'in." His fake accent was awful.

Again their eyes met.

"I'll just see the school marm to her wagon," Mark slurred, as they headed to the parking lot.

Daphne turned to get into the car, accidentally brushing against him. Mark leaned forward. Lightly he kissed her forehead, then withdrew.

"What?" she said.

"What what?" he retorted quickly.

Maybe I shouldn't mix dancing and shooters of Jack Daniels, it's just a little too liberating, Daphne thought as she swung into the driver's seat of her convertible.

Her father was right about work and play. She'd better pay attention to business. But in spite of herself she wondered what it would be like to feel Mark's lips on hers, and then to respond. Heaving a large sigh, she closed her eyes for a moment. "If I do this right," she prayed, "I can make my professional reputation. If I screw up, the company goes into the dumper." It was a giddy feeling to know she was responsible for the business future of her friends. She opened her eyes, waved at Mark, and started the car.

Mark stood beside his Explorer, watching her leave. He slipped into the car. "Son-of-a-bitch." He pounded the steering wheel. In the rear view mirror he could see her taillights disappearing. His near drowning. Linda. Tom. Daphne. The Locator. What else? Was it ordained? Shaking his head, he reflected on the way whiskey brought out the philosopher in him. Most people, for that matter. Thank God Daphne agreed to join them. They didn't have time to wet nurse anyone through another learning curve. Pushing back into the seat, he grinned broadly. "We're going to get there." he nodded, agreeing with himself. "Yeah," he yelled to no one and everyone.

He couldn't wait to be with Linda, to share all the news. If it weren't for Linda, they never would have found Daphne. They would still be struggling in the plant. Strange how everything interconnected. But now . . . He raced to the apartment.

"You smell smokey and boozey," Linda hugged him as he strode through the door. "You should soak in the tub and then tell me all about everything."

"Honey, you just won first prize for mind reading," He shucked off his clothes and pitched them toward the hamper. When he got out of the tub he found Linda already under the sheets in their bed.

Looking up, she noticed him in the doorway. He had a towel draped about his mid-section.

"Show off." She pointed toward a disturbance in the towel.

"Your fault." He strode to the bed, dispensing with the towel as he slipped beneath the sheets.

"Behave yourself for just a minute and tell me what happened."

"Daphne is officially working for us as of today," he whispered in her ear as he trailed a finger down the rim of her other ear.

"That's great." She inched closer to him.

"The weld-fill machine blew up." Again he whispered, this time trailing his finger down her neck.

"That's grea . . . WHAT? Was anyone hurt?" Linda moved away, propping herself up on one elbow.

"No . . . No . . . Just relax." Mark drew her close. "Nobody hurt, just a couple scratches, didn't even need a doctor. But if you're in a nursing mood . . ." One hand crept up below her breast.

"You're terrible," she sighed, nestling closer to him.

"Thank you." His lips brushed hers so lightly they could have been feathers floating on the wind.

"Thank you?" she repeated. She could feel her pulse in her temples.

"If not for your introducing us to Daphne, we might be out of business."

"Sugar?"

"Yes?"

"Tell me later."

CHAPTER TEN
IF IT WERE EASY

"Sorry Mark." Joyce handed him a group of faxes from his investors: *. . . disappointing results . . . concerned about use of funds . . . apparent lack of progress . . . question the present direction of the firm . . . lack of management control . . .*

"They sure aren't throwing roses, are they." Mark scanned the faxes.

. . . under these circumstances we feel a prompt meeting of the shareholders and board of directors at the earliest possible time is mandatory. "The only thing they left out was I should be taken out and shot at sunrise."

Any continuation of funding depended upon the ability of Tom and himself to convince these men that their money was not being wasted. Based upon Daphne's analysis and what Mark saw in the plant, he knew this looked not only difficult but also nearly impossible. They had to have more money, and then they could succeed. But the shareholders wanted success now.

"Joyce, I'll be over at Sean's and then I'll be with Fred Stephens if anyone needs me." He strolled over and gave her a brotherly hug. "It'll be okay."

"Thanks." She smiled weakly, wishing she could share Mark's confidence.

Mark went straight to the hobby shop. The conversation was not what he anticipated.

"So what you're telling me, is that you spent their money, have little to show and they're aggravated." Sean ticked off each item on a finger.

"That's about the size of it."

"That's about normal for an R & D company. Why are they surprised? They are supposedly sophisticated investors. If it were easy, everyone could do it." Sean didn't even blink.

"Normal?"

"Certainly."

"Dare I ask why you never mentioned this little fact to me before?" Mark was nonplussed.

Sean answered immediately, "Every research and development effort I've ever seen, heard of or been a party to, was always a can of worms from start to finish. They always have been and always will be." It was laid out, matter-of-fact, no emotion.

"Every investor knows that, and your investors are sophisticated men, so don't let them whine and cry baby about their money.

"I have no intention of listening to millionaires wimping about their money, but I am responsible for the success or failure of the product. Two different things," said Mark.

"You just answered your own question. It's pointless to try to tell someone in the heat of passion for their idea that it is going to be a hundred times tougher than they imagine. So one simply waits until the moment of truth . . ." Sean walked over to Mark and touched his shoulder calmly, " . . . and then offer whatever help one can." He shook his friend gently.

"If none of us ever had a vision or tried to do the impossible, it would be a pretty rotten world," Sean declared, "so I think it's a lousy idea to shoot down good concepts." But there was more to it than that —something that Tom had said. Sean suspected that things were not all that they appeared. "Have you discussed this with Fred yet?"

"No," said Mark, "but I'm headed up to his house after I

leave here."

"Why?"

Mark sensed Sean knew more than he was willing to say.

"Like you, I trust him and I think a lot of his opinion. I think you should run the entire thing past him. See what he says." Sean smiled and added, "If I can help with anything other than money, which I don't have, just call."

"Okay. Start thinking about photovoltaic cells."

Sean stared at his young friend. Was the stress getting to him or what? "Do you mind if I ask what photovoltaic cells has to do with anything?"

"You may ask, but I have no answer. Humor me." He disappeared down the stairs and headed for Fred's place.

Mark never failed to be impressed by Fred's home. He smelled the ocean breeze as he walked up to the elevated first floor. Looking down past the supporting stilts he could see the parking garages.

"A bit much, for a widower." His engineer's eye figured the home had nearly 4000 square feet of living area. At any rate, the Mercedes looked natural parked beneath the home. Mark thought the Explorer didn't look half bad there either.

"Hi Mark, lets just park in the den for now." He walked ahead. Mark followed quickly. He always liked the den. Some of Fred's best work hung there adjacent to an Audubon plate. The plate, which Fred said had been painted in a remote section of the glades not far from the stilt home, depicted a lone wood Ibis. The birds had long since departed as urban sprawl destroyed habitat. Mark wondered if a similar fate awaited him.

"I was just having some Irish coffee. Will you join me?"

"Yes, thanks." Uneasily Mark sensed a subtle change in Fred's manner.

"Why don't you catch me up on the invention while we enjoy our drinks?" Fred eased into his chair at the desk. "Then you can tell me why you wanted to meet. Or is that the same thing?" He knew damned well it was.

"Uh . . . well, the long and the short of it — I'm having

the best and worst times of my life." Mark stretched out in the comfortable recliner.

Quietly Fred watched him. For a guy in deep trouble he was inexplicably relaxed. Was ignorance bliss? he wondered.

"I've made a couple of . . . well, bad decisions . . . and the result is, we're behind schedule and over budget." He breathed out and waited.

"That's normal for start-ups," Fred responded with a flick of his wrist.

"So I'm told." Quietly, Mark continued. "But I have the feeling that there's a lot going on sort of behind the scenes or out of sight. It makes me uneasy. Maybe I'm just paranoid."

Fred said nothing, but his silence invited conversation.

"I think I have the engineering difficulties under control now. I've hired a new engineer who's working out well. The problem is now with money and investors." Mark looked around uneasily.

Fred sipped his coffee. No expression showed in his eyes.

"I've received faxes from the stockholders, demanding a meeting of the Board of Directors, and a shareholders meeting." Fred did not react. He seemed to take in the news resolutely, not so much as though he already knew it, but simply as though it came as no surprise to him.

"And how do you interpret the faxes?" Fred again lapsed into silence as he nursed his coffee.

"I know something's going on, but I don't know what," Mark continued. "It's upsetting to know the company is in trouble. Although I don't think it's my fault, it is my responsibility." He pondered the truth of the statement. If not his fault, whose?

"Look, I believe I've made the right choices despite the fact that not all of them bore the fruit we wished. I accept full responsibility for that." Pain showed at the corners of his eyes.

He groped for a way to express what he was thinking. "Something else is terribly wrong and I really don't know what to do about it. That's the reason I've come to talk to you, because I know you've been through some tough business deals. If you don't know the answer, at least you may know who to send me to for help."

Fred seemed to muse upon the paintings on the wall. He had carefully thought over how much to tell Mark, since much of what he knew had been obtained in strict confidence. Mark had not yet figured out that Saturn University was a sister operation to Air America. After flying for Air America, Fred had become a Professor at Saturn. His tenure had produced many connections, both government and criminal. Now he felt cornered. If I tell Mark, I may end up with a cement kimono, he brooded. I don't tell him, maybe he gets screwed out of the company. He decided to put Mark on some pathways that would lead him to the answers. Sort of like a mid-term exam in business, except this time if he flunked, he'd lose his butt.

"Mark if I were you, knowing the condition of the firm and the nature of faxes you received from the stockholders, I would expect that the stockholders meeting is not going to be a friendly one."

Mark grinned. That much was obvious.

Fred fiddled with the coffee cup. "I'd do everything I could to put the best possible light on my decisions and choices and behavior. More than that, I'd prepare a rational plan to persuade them to put in more money themselves, or to encourage some of their friends to invest. They may have friends with lots of ready cash. One never knows." He pushed his coffee aside and leaned toward Mark in his chair.

"From what you tell me, you cannot finish the project on the given funds. The choice is between packing the company in, finding someone willing to buy it, which would be very unlikely in its present condition, or finding investment funds or other financing sources to enable you to complete the project." He continued almost conversationally.

"Am I correct, you do not have completed production equipment, you do not have a patent, although you do have a patent pending, and you do not even have a demonstration engineering prototype?" Mark nodded. "How can you show any commercial value?"

Mark flinched. It was all so obvious.

"In fact, without an operating prototype, you can't prove your idea will work and that it can be built. Your original investors obviously came in on their belief in Tom and the prospect of obscene profits. And of course they were satisfied with you sufficiently not to back out of the deal Tom brought them. You are not in a strong position to sell the company.

"From a return on investment viewpoint, since it's going to cost several times the amount originally forecast, it's going to be tough to convince the investors that a strong return is still possible. They might even be better off to simply write off their investments. One must suspect that the return has been greatly compromised."

"We're working on that," Mark interrupted briefly.

"If I were an investor I would need some rational reason to believe that there was something different that would allow me to still recover my investment and make the projected return I was expecting or hoping to make." He returned his gaze to Mark.

"All that is true." Mark agreed.

"In all fairness to you, I believe you made it clear that this was risk capital and these men could lose all or a part of their investment if the project should fail."

Mark nodded his head affirmatively.

"Even so, investors do not like to see their capital pissed down a hole so to speak. Frankly, I don't think you'll have an easy task getting more money or more time." His shoulders squared, he leveled his gaze upon Mark.

"There are some other things you should be asking yourself. Why did the shareholders call the meeting? What information were they acting on and where did it come from? If it didn't come from you, is it accurate? You need to think along those lines." He saw understanding in Mark's eyes.

"And finally, I think you better explore not only the technical problems you've got, but also what progress you've made in marketing, what progress you've made with the government if any, and whether or not there might be the potential for other sources of financing, such as Small Business Administration,

DARPA or an SBIR. You need to examine every option before the meeting. This is what I tried to warn you about before. This is business."

Mark leaned back, savoring the coffee more than the brandy strengthening it. Never had he appreciated Fred more than at this moment.

"I thank you." He gazed directly into Fred's eyes, sensing pain and concern. "Don't worry, I learned a couple of things, maybe I've been rode hard but I'm not through yet."

The tightness left Fred's face.

"I'm going to make this thing fly not only for me, but for Linda, and for the stockholders. It's not just about that. I have been in the water. I know what it means to be scared shitless wondering if the sharks are going to get to you before a rescue boat arrives. I know what it feels like to know the water is absorbing the last bit of your body heat." His green eyes blackened. "Some way, I'm going to get a product into the hands of these SCUBA divers, these fishermen, to everyone who needs it, so that if God forbid they wind up in the same position I was in, they'll have a fighting chance of being found alive. And not just by accident or dumb luck, as I was." He struck the desk.

Suddenly Mark felt self-conscious. He realized he sounded like a preacher. How incongruous for the student to be lecturing the professor. Yet he felt these things so strongly that even if he'd chosen not to, they had to be said.

Fred started as Mark's fist pounded on the desk. Inside, he defended the rush of feelings that he was struggling to hide. Hell, it was normal to be proud of Mark now. This was how Billy would have behaved under similar circumstances.

For a few minutes the two sat without speaking. Finally Fred broke the silence. "Listen son, I'm not going to blow any smoke up your ass, you got a tough job ahead of you, but I believe in you and I think you can do it. Just give it your best shot." He gave Mark an even-tempered glance and rose, indicating the conference was over. They trailed toward the front door.

"Thanks for everything, really." Warmly Mark gripped Fred's hand.

In an unexpected gesture, Fred held Mark's shoulder and gave him an affectionate shake. "Hang tough son."

"Thanks."

On the long drive to Lauderdale, Mark turned on the radio. "When you're dealt 'em down and dirty," crooned the country singer, "you take it like a man, because the heart is all that matters in the end." Perfect, he thought. It comforted him the way country music seemed to cut through the bull and get to the soul of a matter.

"Watch your step," Joyce cautioned as Mark walked into the office. Before she could explain, he heard a clattering sound from the rear of the plant. "Daphne." Joyce pointed toward the work area.

Mark eased open the door. He peered into the factory. Daphne was bending over to recover something from the floor.

"Ahoy. Anyone home?" Mark prepared the way.

"What does it look like?" she snarled, spinning around.

Mark hesitated before answering. Daphne was holding a shattered Locator in her hands.

"Well. It looks like someone is in a high state of pissatude." He flashed a conciliatory smile. "It also looks like someone needs to remember we share problems around here."

Daphne dropped her head and snorted a half-apologetic, "Yes. Dammit. It does." Raising her head, Daphne returned Mark's smile. "Okay, we have a problem."

"What else is new?"

"No. I mean if you want to stick this little surprise," she waved the Locator at him, "in someone's ear at the shareholder's meeting, we have a problem."

Mark reached out and grasped the Locator. "Valve failed."

She nodded.

"Cutting through all the crap, what are the odds of one of these hummers working?"

"Not better than 50-50." She heaved a sigh and flung up her arms.

Mark placed the Locator on a bench, then moved next to Daphne. Gently, he placed his hands on her shoulders. "That's a hundred percent better than no chance." He backed away. "Without the improvements you've made, we'd have zero chance of a successful demonstration. So, Madam Engineer, lighten up on yourself."

"But . . ."

"No but's."

Mark's warm green eyes reassured Daphne. Somehow she would give him a working prototype. "You go manage, and let me engineer. I'll be all right." She motioned toward the door.

He headed back to his office. Mark's stomach knotted, as he replayed her words, "Not better than 50-50." Shaking off such thoughts, he strode to his office. He had much to do.

CHAPTER ELEVEN
SURPRISE SURPRISE

Monday morning everyone showed up for the stockholders meeting. It had been set in a hotel near the expressway and Cypress Creek Road, comfortable and convenient for the out-of-town stockholders, with outstanding food and easy access to the shopping malls.

Mark was dressed for combat in his blue pinstripe suit, white shirt and maroon tie.

Promptly at 10:30 he started. "Good morning, I am Mark Hansen and we're ready to begin the meeting of the shareholders of Locator."

"Let me introduce Mr. Benjamin Tenney, the corporate council, who will do the honors this morning."

The meeting began innocently with the introduction of the various stockholders to each other and to members of the group.

"Now, Mark, if you would recap the company's progress for all of us." Ben made a sweeping motion. He sat next to Tom.

Mark thought, If this were Kuwait, I'd be looking for land mines.

He passed out the company financials. "There's not a lot of good news in this Balance Sheet, and obviously there's no income on the Income Statement." Mark noticed that in addition to the company attorney, two other lawyers were there with their investors.

He made his initial report brief, concise and brutally to the point. "I must call your attention to the fact that the production machinery is not complete. The patent application was filed, but of course has not been issued at this early time. Our marketing efforts will be reported by Tom Garret. As you already know, most of the investment money has been spent and a considerable amount of additional funds will be required to complete the project." He delivered the information in a monotone.

At this point he turned the meeting over to Tom. What followed was not pleasant; neither did it come as a shock.

"Fellow shareholders," Tom swept the room with his eyes, "we're in this situation together. Many of you are here because of my recommendation that you invest in the company." He paused. "It is my unpleasant duty to tell you that because of lack of proper selection and guidance of engineering personnel, and the resultant poor progress in design and development, it has been impossible to do any effective marketing or any effective work with the government." Tom glanced at Mark.

"The company is in dire straits essentially because of underestimates of the cost and difficulty of the project. Operations are primarily Mr. Hansen's responsibility, however."

Jack Jankowski, a tall neatly dressed man, rose in the back of the room. "Tom, if you'll pardon my interrupting. It seems what this boils down to is you and your young friend are trying to tell us we have little to show for the money but an application to protect a product that does not exist. No one can deny the burden of mismanagement rests on Mark's shoulders."

Tom winced. "Jack, I think that's a little harsh."

Mark was irritated more than surprised. It had been shareholders' pressure that had caused the choice to shift to an older more experienced person, who had just happened to be a man. He retook the podium.

"First, let me thank Tom for his comments and explanations. Jack, I can readily understand why anyone confronted with the stated facts would certainly have reached the same conclusion." He turned and partially bowed in acknowledgement. "However, there are some additional pieces of information you may wish to consider that will enable you to reach a comprehensive and realistic understanding of the situation." Mark pulled out several stacks of paper.

Pausing, Mark smiled out over his audience. "Lee Iacoocca confronted a situation much like this when he bailed out Chrysler. He saw something in the company that few others were able to see. Although I would never liken Locator to Chrysler, nor myself to Mr. Iacoocca, I would hope that after you've had a chance to review the facts you will agree with me that our company has a credible future.

"Let's look at the financial projections, cost vs. returns, the sales projections, and the return on investment projections." He paused, allowing his comment to sink in and curiosity to build.

"Given certain changes, it is still possible to reach the initial projections despite the great increase in capital required. There are two reasons for this." Mark then passed out drawings of Daphne's new design and his new financials.

"Notice the reduced cost projection and the increased sales estimates. As you see, gentlemen, by a product redesign and some engineering changes, the cost of manufacture will be reduced by 37%. We had to make the product a little larger and heavier, but the substantial reduction in retail price will greatly increase sales."

Much rumbling of paper. Mark hesitated while the investors looked at the financials. Calmly he sipped from the water glass at the podium.

"As you can see, not only will this produce the expected rate of return on investment, it will also produce a 1.7% increase in ROI. We trust that will not hurt your feelings, nor those of your accountants." Mark delivered the message with a smile. It was received by many skeptical frowns.

"That of course was the good news. The bad news is also right in front of you. We will require an additional capital infusion of $450,000 to get to the market place with the product and probably an additional $250,000 for marketing and cash flow until the income stream from sales starts to carry the company."

The new figures were met by a mixture of disbelief, dismay and distrust. Only the lawyers were impassive. You bastards could care less, thought Mark. No wonder. You get paid win or lose.

Tom seemed puzzled, but Benjamin Tenney, the company attorney who was seated next to Tom, asked to be recognized.

Elegant in his charcoal gray three-piece suit, Benjamin marched to the front of the room and took the podium. "We all recognize the youthful enthusiasm that our operating manager has, but with all due respect, let me point out that these figures are based on two unreasonable, illogical assumptions that appear more wishful thinking than he would care to admit." Benjamin frowned deprecatingly at Mark.

"First there is no evidence that the current management can even produce the original product, much less this revised product. Second, the sales figures are based on cost factors that are pipe dreams. They are not the result of the mature consideration of an experienced production manager or marketing professional."

The lawyer hesitated, doing a quick reading of the room. The air was tense. "It's clear that the company is in trouble because of just such immature management practices. It would be my suggestion as company attorney and member of the Board of Directors, that the shareholders exercise their options as provided in the shareholders' agreement. I recommend you take back the stock holdings of Mark and Tom and redistribute them for sale, so as to raise funds to hire a competent manager and engineer who will be able to complete the product development and get it to the market." Confidently he strode back to his chair.

The room was silent as a cemetery. All eyes focused on Mark. They reminded Mark of a pack of lemon sharks eyeing a bleeding grouper.

Mark rose, smiling broadly. "Why thank you Ben, for your kind thoughts about youth and enthusiasm." He then passed out the certified cost estimates from suppliers. "Ben, I'm sure these will make you feel much better."

Scowling, Ben snatched the papers.

Mark continued, "As you will observe, gentlemen, we have gotten a little past the dream stage. These are only estimates, but these suppliers are reputable and reliable and the estimates before you are certified for 90 days with a 5% cap on increases for 9 months. If this is pie in the sky, I will gladly have a slice, thank you very much."

The shareholders stared at Ben.

"As to the matter of recalling my shareholding, I wouldn't recommend trying that." His cold green eyes focused on Ben. "You will notice in the package I just handed you, there is a legal opinion, prepared by my attorneys, about the questionable wisdom of unlawfully extracting my stock, and the legal consequences if you imprudently made such an attempt."

Flushing visibly, Ben Tenney jumped up from his chair sending it backwards as he strode past the agitated shareholders. He marched to the podium, forcefully sharing it with Mark. Although his legal training allowed him to retain control, it was only by a force of will.

Ben peered at Mark over his reading glasses. "These papers are all well and good. You may have the seed of an idea here, but the fact remains that you have spent nearly a half a million dollars with nothing material to show for it." Disdainfully he tossed the papers on the podium.

Doubt and anger permeated the room.

"Further, I, of course, will want to review your attorneys' legal opinion," he sputtered, obviously running out of energy and ideas, "since this all comes as a surprise to me."

Mark kept his composure, and with elaborate politeness, said, "I am grateful that you can see some merit in the work my new engineer has done," nodding toward Ben, " and in the financial analysis I developed." Again he half bowed in feigned respect.

"It is gratifying that you would like to review, respectfully I am sure, the legal opinions of my attorneys." He smiled pointedly at Jack and Ben.

Ben squirmed nervously.

"As to your misgivings about the practicality of our proposal, you had only to ask and we would gladly have shown you the operating engineering prototypes we developed as proofs of concept."

Shocked disbelief flashed across Ben's face. The attorney looked questioningly into Tom's eyes. What could the kid be up to? As he adjusted his tie casually, Ben sized up the shareholders. The room's noise level rose as chairs were shifted, and brief interchanges sprang up.

Mark pulled his briefcase from the shelf on the podium. Stillness settled upon the room. "Naturally," he started, "we will prepare similar clear plastic demonstration units for use as marketing tools." With that, Mark opened his briefcase, removed the hand-built prototype he, Daphne and Sean had constructed, took off the plastic top, pulled the red inflating handle. He said a silent prayer as he waited the split seconds before the valve opened. Then he watched as the inflatable radar reflector filled.

"Psssssssshhhhhhhhhhhft." The hissing sound of the helium gas filling the balloon was the only sound in the room. Mark removed the retainer clip, allowing the balloon to silently and quickly rise to the ceiling of the room. In stunned silence the shareholders and their attorneys comprehended what they had witnessed. The glistening balloon innocently bobbed against the ceiling.

Realizing he had failed in his power play, Ben steeled himself to accept the consequences.

"Gentlemen," said Mark, "we know we have a product that will be a winner. It is our hope that you will take this opportunity to renew your investments in the company and reap the benefits of our mutual success. If, however, you decide not to extend your participation, I will accept your decisions with no hard feeling on my side. Meeting adjourned. Thank you very much."

"You dragged me half way around the world from an important meeting so I could watch you publicly make an ass of yourself?" hissed Jack to Ben Tenney. "Tell your Mr. Adams to kiss my ass."

Abruptly the attorney left the podium and strode to where Tom was reviewing Mark's proposal. "What the hell's going on here?" he barked at Tom. "I don't enjoy getting my butt kicked by some punk kid." His head flipped in Mark's direction.

"You didn't know about that . . . that . . . balloon?"

Ben realized his mistake as Tom uncoiled from the chair, dumping the papers on the floor. "Listen, you lilac-smelling twit, I'm just as surprised as you are. But I'm not going to piss in my pants just because the kid was a little smarter than you gave him credit for." Tom glanced back at the podium. Mark was silently putting the proto in his briefcase. Why wasn't he smiling, Tom wondered.

Remorse was all Mark could feel because he'd been forced to keep a secret from his partner. He could not risk Tom being involved in the power play. Events implied he was right. The damage was done. Tom's relationship with the shareholders probably was beyond repair. And probably was Mark's as well. Cynically Mark thought to himself, it's just business.

Mark picked up his briefcase and walked toward the door, trailing the balloon in his wake. At the door, he turned and faced the shareholders' group. "Good day." It sounded like goodbye.

Well Bucky, he consoled himself, *you kept the sharks away, but we're still in mighty stormy waters.* The balloon trailed behind him. *Fortune sure favors the bold.* He looked back at the shareholders. *If they only knew. What the hell, a 50 percent chance was better than no chance at all.*

As he strode toward Linda, he reflected, we can forget the present investors as a source of funding. At least they're no longer openly hostile. He still could not understand their attitudes.

Sean sidled up and whispered, "You wily rascal, I just love it!" He added, "Sorry about Tom."

"Yeah, me too."

"Well people." Triumphantly he addressed Linda and Daphne, "we deserve lunch." Turning to Paul and Sean, "all of us."

"I've seen some high stakes poker games," said Paul, "but that hand . . . I would have loved to watch."

Mark put down his briefcase, hugged Linda and Daphne and shook hands with Sean and Paul. "Lunch is on me."

"Damn right it is." Paul and Sean were sanguine in their reactions. They'd seen companies born and die. They'd been present at too many celebrations and too many wakes to be overly involved emotionally, but they did have an investment in time, energy and faith. Inside, they were pleased for Mark when they witnessed the confusion and dismay of the lawyers and shareholders as they exited the meeting.

"Don't you just love it?" Paul asked Mark.

"Not all of it," Mark responded, thinking about the confused look on Tom's face as he exited the room.

Sean felt particularly bad since he'd introduced the two and had been the initiator of the partnership which suffered in the meeting. It had been too easy after all, he reflected.

"Come on Daphne, you should be dancing on the tabletops after what you accomplished," Linda bubbled enthusiastically.

"Oh, I'm happy, I'm just worn out, that's all," Daphne replied uneasily. Linda didn't understand the technical and financial hurdles still facing Mark and the rest.

Like Sean, Daphne was also sad that Tom had to be kept in the dark. It had looked like he was involved in the shareholder problem. She knew much would change at the plant because of that.

"You guys wouldn't be so hungry right now if that bitch had failed to inflate," laughed Paul.

"Amen!" Mark agreed.

"Now all we have to do is find sources of investment capital for a high risk, high return venture." Mark grinned and squeezed Linda's hand.

"Is that all?" Paul interrupted with a massive fist pounding on the table and several indistinguishable expletives.

"Guys, I just met a wild guy from New Zealand you've got to talk to. He was just in the Keys fishing with me and was telling me about what troubles they have when anyone gets lost at sea in Australia or New Zealand." Mark looked intently into the big man's face.

"You know they don't have a paid professional coast guard like we do, so when they're in trouble, they're really in trouble. The guy is well connected in the government, and he's connected with money people there. I don't know if he has money of his own or if he would go for a deal, but I think he's a good shot to try."

He tossed down his drink, then drew his hand across his mouth in a wiping motion. "More wine," he bellowed.

"More wine," echoed Daphne and Linda, lifting their empty glasses in a salute to Mark. The rest followed suit.

"Let's try to arrange for a preliminary discussion," suggested Mark. "Paul, would you first simply run the concept by the fellow to see if there's any interest at all?"

"Sure, no sweat."

At last Mark leaned back in the chair. Daphne observed his calm green eyes playing over Linda's face. A devilish smile crept across his lips and he leaned forward to whisper something into her ear.

Smiling, Linda brushed Mark gently. Then, catching Daphne's gaze, she remarked, "Men. You can't take them anywhere."

During the lunch other names were brought up and other paths explored, but only two seemed to hold promise. One would be the fellow in New Zealand, and the other would be Walt, Sean's friend from Japan.

When Mark and Daphne returned to the plant after lunch, they were greeted by Tom who was waiting in the lobby. He walked up to Mark after acknowledging Daphne's presence with a nod, and said, "Hey, how come you didn't tell me about the prototype?"

Hesitantly Mark replied, "Tom I really didn't know if it would work. I took a chance, and if the demonstration had failed I didn't want you to share in my humiliation. You would have been in a position to disavow any knowledge of the failed prototype. I think it's called plausible deniability. And frankly, after the arguments and shareholder problems, I wondered if you might be involved in the meeting."

"On the one hand I can see why you thought that way, but I'm disappointed you didn't talk to me about it. I think it would be real hard to work together now." The last words trailed off into silence as Tom appraised Mark, wondering how much he really knew.

"I feel bad about it too, Tom. But we both did what we thought was right."

Agreeing with a nod, Tom went on, "Under the circumstances, I think it better if I make room for someone else to handle the marketing." He flashed an ingratiating grin. "No hard feelings Mark. I wish you and Daphne the best. Don't forget, if you succeed, my stock becomes valuable."

"No hard feelings. And I hope we all get rich." Mark meant it all.

Pausing at the door Tom added, "I'll be willing to work for a week or two to make any transition easier, but I'm going to accept an offer as a consultant in Australia, so I'd prefer to leave as soon as it's convenient."

"No problem. And best of luck." Again, Mark meant it all.

"What the heck," Mark reasoned, "you would've found it necessary to leave anyway because of the financial condition of the company. I just regret it's under these circumstances. Who knows, our paths may yet cross again."

"Could be. It's a small planet." The door eased shut.

CHAPTER TWELVE
HOBO SOUP

Daphne read his thoughts. "Just as well. If Tom had joined with the unhappy stockholders, his people would have put more money into the company. Tom would have been left in charge of the company and in a strong position to make money when the product hit the market, if it ever did."

"A big if." Linda, who had kept quiet, knew that only Daphne and Mark could get the product to market.

"Amen." Mark felt he could rely on Daphne for the technical expertise to complete the production equipment. He could handle the patent and administration.

"Before we break our arms patting ourselves on the back, we've got some major hustling to do. We've got to find someone to handle the marketing. It won't mean a damn to build'em if we can't sell'em. Aside from not having a patent, operating equipment or capital, we're in good shape." Raising the capital would be a bitch. The present book value of the company was well below what had been invested so far.

"So, what's the plan?" asked Linda.

"The parade of the bankers," answered Mark, smiling grimly. The parade was not restricted to bankers, but would include lawyers, financial brokers, and venture capital people—anyone who would listen.

"Mark, are you on a diet?" Joyce teased her boss.

"Not exactly," he muttered looking at the orange in front of him.

"You just haven't had as much practice at being broke as I have." She smiled.

"Well not lately, anyway." Shaking his head, he thought back to his senior year at the University of Miami. "Do you know what hobo soup is?"

"No, you have me there."

"When I was in school and was really broke, we'd go to Royal Castle. A friend worked there and would give us hot water. We'd mix in some mustard, ketchup and pickle relish and make . . ."

"Hobo soup." Joyce laughed.

"You got it." He nodded. "On a good day we even got left-over crackers."

Joyce looked around. "Promise not to tell." Mark nodded. "When I was in school and we were real broke, we'd go to the Coke machines and get the empty bottles and go cash them in."

Mark looked at Joyce in disbelief. "Get outta here."

"I swear."

"Well, I don't know how to tell you this. But if things keep going the way they are now, both of us may be chasing empties and living on hobo soup." He rested a reassuring hand on hers. "But not yet. Stick with me kid, I've got an orange tree."

Mark whirled around in his chair and from the credenza produced a small bag of oranges.

"Nope, I hate oranges. You'll just have to grab one of those bankers and turn him upside down and shake him."

"I'll do my best," he joked, "I hope you and Daphne can work in the dark, because the power company may give us the opportunity to experience roughing it like our forefathers. I hocked my photographic equipment to cover the phone bill, and I'm tap city."

"Well you can't scare me off," retorted Joyce. "I want to hear the excuse you whip on one of those banking dudes if they show up and the power's off."

"I haven't used the old 'lightning struck the transformer and we have no power' excuse. And I've been saving 'the materials shipments were late so they sent the employees home' routine," Mark joked.

Joyce shook her head and looked at the little plaque on Mark's desk. "Don't Let Nothin' But Fear Hold You Back." It had been a gift from Sean.

One day Daphne had cornered Mark away from their friends. "Mark, I'll make you a deal. My folks still consider me a student so I can forego my pay, but with the understanding I get my full consulting fee and I'm taken care of, if and when we get the company up and running."

"Where do I find you people?" Mark hugged her, lifting her off her feet.

"Can I take that as a yes?" she managed breathlessly.

As for Linda, she too could rely on her parents at least for a few months. Mark found himself working what amounted to two jobs, modeling as often as he could find work, and then hustling to keep the project going.

"This looks like an old Chaplin film," Linda joked to Daphne and Joyce. "Mark runs by in a bathing suit to do a commercial, then slips into a business suit to do the sincere businessman for a potential investor." She shook her head. "I don't know how he keeps going."

When she repeated this to Mark that evening he replied, "It's easy. A year ago I worked enough to keep my bar tab and expenses under control. Now I'm having a good time building our future. Come over here," he beckoned to her, "and we'll build some future."

Linda snuggled closer and removed the drink from his hand.

For potential investors who visited the plant, everything was expertly staged. Linda acted as an employee and Mark would be the operating executive. On special occasions they would recruit Sean, Paul or any other warm bodies they could hustle, and place them strategically in what appeared to be logical activities to enhance the impression of a viable enterprise.

Only once did Linda catch Mark looking dejectedly out his window. "I love you," she whispered across the office.

"Sorry, Honey." He swung around in the chair. "I love you too. I guess I'm just a little down. I really thought the guy from Zurich was going to invest." He looked at the failed Locator sample before him. "You just had to crap-out right in front of the guy, didn't you?" Mark picked up the unit, briefly examined it, and then tossed it into the wastebasket.

Somehow they survived.

Daphne was steadily improving the prototypes. But even though they now worked almost 70% of the time, it seemed that the failures inevitably occurred at the worst possible moment, dooming a promising campaign to the dumpster.

Mark's phone rang. "You know Babe Ruth led in strikeouts as well as home runs," Gordon Hansen rasped across the wires to his son. Mark wanted to throw up. He knew that. He forced a smile. " . . . and Edison failed thousands of times before he succeeded in developing a commercial light bulb." His dad was trying to help — now. As desperate as he was, he could not bring himself to ask his dad for money. He'd rather eat hobo soup.

"Abe Lincoln failed many times before being elected . . ." Mark had no illusions about success. He knew that only a failure of will would seal the doom of the project.

"Thanks, Dad." He was ready to hang up. "And say hi to the folks for me." Mark replaced the phone and sat looking at the receiver. Maybe he should've asked for the money. Gordon Hansen was comfortably fixed – no. He just couldn't ask his father. The way he'd left . . .

The phone rang again and Mark almost let it ring, then relented.

"Locator. May I help you?"

"Hell, no," was the reply, "but maybe I can help you." It was Sean. "Remember my Desert Storm buddy, Walt, I was telling you about. He's passing through Lauderdale on the way to a meeting in Houston and would like to meet you."

"Sure, glad to."

"He might be interested in the Locator."

"Make that very glad to."

"One thing." Sean seemed reluctant. "I know you probably already understand this, but it's considered bad form in Japan to jump into a business conversation. I wouldn't bring up business unless Walt does first. Okay?"

"Hey guy, Walt doesn't sound Japanese and I don't know anything about Japanese culture, but I wouldn't do that anyway. I don't want to appear overanxious. Fred says that's the kiss of death."

"Fred's a bright guy. And I did think about photovoltaic. But what does that have to do with anything?"

"Yes."

"What do you mean yes? What about it — photovoltaic?"

"If I were to aim an X-ray at a photovoltaic cell, what do you think would happen?"

"Nothing."

"Nothing?"

"Well, no voltage would be produced. And probably the silicon wafer would be degraded by the X-ray."

"The X-ray would ruin the cell and no voltage would be produced. Right?"

"Yeah. Why?" Sean's curiosity was at a boil.

"Nothing. Just thinking."

"Fat chance. See ya." Sean stared at the phone, wondering what could possibly be distracting Mark's attention from the emergency locator. More importantly, he wondered how Mark and Walt would get along. His answer was soon in coming.

"Mark, I'd like you to meet my amigo, Walt."

"I've heard a lot about you, Walt. Nice to meet you."

"Why don't we cruise on down to the restaurant and talk there?" Sean suggested.

"Good idea, been awhile since I ate American." Walt led the group toward the door.

"Nice threads," Sean remarked, admiring Walt's clothes. He was dressed in casual but expensive clothing, nice European-style leather slippers.

Mark wondered if he were still connected with the government. His fine-textured deep brown hair was neat and cut short. "How did you wind up in Japan?"

"I spent some R & R time in Tokyo, I liked it and decided to stay for a while. Being small is a benefit in Japan."

Mark found it easy to imagine him blending in with Japanese businessmen. Even his nose was smaller than a typical Anglo. Mark was aware that Japanese called Anglos "big noses." In exchange, the Japanese were called "slant eyes."

"So you guys knew each other in the Mid-East?" Mark inquired.

"Yeah, Walt was involved in some special warfare stuff. He was the perfect instructor because he knew all the toys and he's quite a linguist."

"Well you did O.K. yourself, Seansan." Walt shot back.

"I knew how to ask where the latrine was and how deep should we dig in," Sean grinned.

"Good things to know." Mark shook his head.

"Mark, I understand from Sean that you're interested in science. I too share such interests."

"Yes, in what field?"

"Mostly mariculture. My clients got me interested. As you know, there is almost no arable land in Japan and almost no remaining natural resources."

"Then food production is their most difficult problem?"

"No, actually it is energy and pollution that are most troublesome. We thought nuclear would be the answer, but with earthquakes . . ."

"So the island nation looks to the sea for the answers?" Mark queried.

"Yes."

"A very industrious people, I hear," Mark added.

Walt smiled. "Don't believe everything you read about Japan. We don't work all the time. We also look to the sea for recreation."

"I enjoy scuba diving." Mark decided that once thrown, it's best to get right back on the horse. "I'm planning a photographic dive off a wreck near Marathon in the Keys when I can make a little time."

"How interesting." Walt noticeably brightened. "I'm a scuba instructor. If it wouldn't be an intrusion, I would love to dive the wrecks."

"Great idea. I'll try to set it up."

Sean was pleased with himself. The conversation was guaranteed for the day. By the time they returned to the hobby shop he was well satisfied that the introduction had taken.

"Mark, you have a message to call the plant." Barbara handed him a note.

"Excuse me a minute, gentlemen."

"Sean, where did you find this man with manners?" Walt was used to the typical American brash approach to business. Mark was a pleasant surprise.

"We play a bit of soccer."

"It might be possible to introduce him to my Japanese partners without loss of face. It will be interesting to see how he handles himself in the ocean," he said prophetically. Sean had already told Walt of the close call in Bimini.

Mark returned from the phone." Gentlemen, you'll have to excuse me, but I have to get back to the plant." He didn't share the information with Sean, but Daphne had discovered a problem with the balloon manufacturing process and she was concerned about how they would solve it.

"Walt, look forward to doing some diving."

"I also." He bowed slightly.

CHAPTER THIRTEEN
REPRIEVE

When Mark arrived at the plant, he checked in with Joyce.

"No good news, just bills."

"Just leave them on my desk, I'll look them over later." He could look a long time, he thought grimly; he just couldn't pay them. Determined not to let these irritations get him down, he went out to the factory floor to talk to Daphne. He found her near the balloon machine.

The machine was about twenty feet long and four feet wide. On one end it had two steel cages on wheels that supported two rolls of the laminated balloon material. A few feet from the rolls, mounted upon the table, was a plastic welding machine.

"Hi Boss," she greeted him knowing how it annoyed him to be called that. "This connector's not sealing to the balloon material. I'm stumped." She held out a sample.

This time it was her butt on the line. The manufacturer had told her that the machine couldn't do what she wanted it to. "Despite the factory disclaimer, an engineering Professor Andy Parkmon, assures me it'll work. He even spent the best part of six hours last night trying to tweak the plastic welder to get a good bond." She looked exasperated.

"That's in addition to the 25 or 30 hours you already spent?" he asked solicitously.

"Yes. It's looking bad. I spent ten thousand dollars we don't have for this little hummer," she patted the sonic machine, "and if it doesn't work, we're screwed."

"And?" Mark asked.

"So far, I checked out the balloon material which might be at fault. Mr. Chin, their factory representative, met me today and explored the possibilities." She tugged at a sample of the material. "We checked samples for thickness, conductivity, durability and heat sensitivity. There was no indication that the balloon material was at fault. He feels the plastic in the connector is the problem."

"Hummmm. Chin has a vested interest in not finding his company's product at fault." Mark picked at the material.

Daphne exhaled heavily. "I know." Mark saw the strain reflected in her eyes. She continued evenly, "But his education in materials science and particularly plastics, led him to think there was an additive in the plastic that was interfering with the weld." Daphne concurred. "At last I concluded he was right, that something must be wrong with the connector. I trust his integrity. He could be wrong, but I don't think so."

Daphne picked up a plastic part, briefly rotated it, and then slammed it down upon the bench. "The thing that infuriates me is that I already checked with Mr. Bronson, the plastic molder, and he assured me the material was as specified."

Mark flinched. Her anger surprised him.

"I trusted him, but I'm so sure he is wrong, I insisted that he double check with the plastic manufacturer."

"If you're right they've cost us several weeks of wasted time as well as a lot of money," Mark scowled. He snatched the connector from the bench. "Daphne, there's something fishy about this. I should tell Bronson to eat crap and die, but their bill is past due. It is hard to beat up on someone about quality when you owe them money."

Daphne stood up and reached to retrieve the valve. "You're such a softie, Mark. Peter would use the questionable quality of this plastic as an excuse for late payment, and make them feel guilty." She pitched the connector toward a wastebasket. Mark hardly noticed as the plastic clattered into the basket.

"If it's none of my business, say so." She hesitated, then continued, "but I think something else is eating you, not the welding. Want to talk about it?" She leaned back against the bench.

"You've been around me too much," Mark sighed, "you're starting to read my mind." As he looked at her, Daphne silently averted her eyes and picked up the sample balloon material.

"Did I tell you the connector supplier is one of three companies that want to force us into Involuntary Bankruptcy?" He was sure he hadn't.

"No. Why would they do that?" Now she faced him directly, her anger matching his. She was stunned. They had such a good business relationship and it made no sense to her.

"Damn good question." Mark shook his head and angrily kicked the wastebasket. "Like to hear what they said?"

"Does a wild boar dump in the woods?"

"They don't want to hurt us, they said, but they're under pressure to collect, and other business considerations were forcing them to be tough." He struck the balloon machine with his fist.

"Do you believe that crap? He just bought a new Gulfstream II, cash flow ain't no way a problem. Their attorneys told them it was their best bet at collecting, since they would quickly get through the court process, whereas if they sued in civil court, it might be two years before they were heard."

"After we get out of this, I hope he and his bankruptcy buddies will enjoy it when we take our business to other suppliers."

Mark looked grimly at the welder.

"What really pisses me off is that they're right. Between us, I was relying on the slowness of the civil process for a little breathing room until we could raise additional capital."

Daphne shook her head. "That doesn't explain their attitude, does it?"

"No. I never in my worst nightmare foresaw that anyone would play hardball like this." Mark raised both hands to his head and smoothed back his hair. "Damn." Slowly he exhaled.

"On the recommendation of Ordean, I've talked to a bankruptcy law specialist. He advised me that all we needed to do was settle with one of the three petitioners. If we could, they won't meet the minimum requirements for an Involuntary Bankruptcy petition."

"Can we settle with Bronson?"

"One tiny problem, the bill is $12,000. I've used my savings, Linda has scrounged all she can, and you're already working on the if-come." He summoned a grim smile.

"With all the technical crap on your mind, I didn't want to distract you with this stuff." He forced a grin, which rapidly faded. "This will probably sound paranoid. But these people are going way beyond normal. Usually any of the three suppliers would have taken partial good faith payments and been satisfied. Suddenly all three are going for our throat."

Mark couldn't put his finger on it, but something had changed in the relationship with Randy Bronson. He thought of his last conversation with him. He wasn't angry, which Mark would've understood. Just over and over, "I'm sorry Mark. There's nothing I can do. It's out of my hands. I must have all the money now."

"What it boils down to is that we have to find a way to settle with at least one of the petitioners to head off a total shutdown and liquidation of the company." Mark finished uneasily.

Daphne swore under her breath and came over to Mark. "Are you all right?" Anxiously she searched his face. "You just told me we're on the brink of doom and you don't even look worried."

"Been around Sean too much, I guess." Mark shook his head, smiling ruefully at her. He picked up a shop cloth and idly wiped off the welder. "Sons of bitches can't kill us and can't eat us."

She wanted to say, "Don't be too sure," but remained silent.

"Hold the fort a bit," Mark abruptly headed for the door. "I'm going to see if I can shake loose some help." Mark had set a meeting with Fred, hoping he would be able to suggest a way to juggle the situation until he could raise the needed capital. He couldn't approach Sean, who had already made it clear he could help with anything but money.

Mark parked in the lot near Fred's studio on Worth Avenue in Palm Beach. For the first time he thought how out-of-place the Explorer looked among the BMW's and Rolls. He paused to enjoy the beautiful Spanish architecture. "How did he do it?" Mark wondered again. Sure, he made good money doing portraits, even commercial work. Even so . . . his life style . . .

Fred was just wrapping up a session when Mark entered.

"Yvonne, this is Mark Hansen." The striking fair-skinned girl acknowledged him with a nod.

He returned her nod. "I saw your *Vanity* cover. Very nice." Her blonde hair played a stunning counterpoint to the black silk scarf draped around her shoulders. It was her only attire.

Yvonne quickly refocused her attention on the job at hand. She appeared to have excellent focus.

"That's a wrap." Fred shut down the lights.

Yvonne gathered her gear. For the first time Mark noticed a white bird with a strange yellow plume on its forehead quietly waiting on the arm of a chair. Unperturbed, it watched Mark and Fred. Yvonne offered her finger and the bird hopped aboard, then walked up her arm to perch on one shoulder. Fred whispered something to her, then came toward the office.

"I didn't know you were a bird fancier," Mark said.

"I enjoy stroking my cockatoo." She laughed over her shoulder as she exited.

I'd bet on it, said Mark to himself.

"Want a Pepsi?" Fred offered, "or Perrier with a twist?"

"Perrier is fine." Smiling, "There was a time I would have swapped the Explorer for one of these." He lifted the glass and stared briefly into the bubbling water.

"By the way you look, maybe I should have offered you some Jack Daniels." Fred sat on the corner of his desk, eyeing his friend. "Why don't you tell me all about it?"

Mark sank into an overstuffed chair. "If I was paranoid about the shareholders, then I'm surely nuts now. Some things are going on that make no sense." Mark filled in his friend on the unexpected and unpleasant turn of events.

Fred noted that Mark didn't whimper or whine as some people do when faced with adversity. He laid down the facts in an almost emotionless tone.

"Do you feel the creditors are to blame for your present situation?" Fred slid off the desk. He stood looking down at Mark.

"Absolutely not." Emphatically he shook his head. "It's my responsibility."

"Yes it is," Fred agreed.

Mark raised both hands. He studied the palms, then raised his eyes. "How they're reacting is what baffles me."

A partial smile traced Fred's lips. "If they called you and told you what a scumbag you are for not paying promptly — that, you'd understand." He moved behind the desk.

"All right, it sounds silly . . . but yes I would. It's this almost puppet-like response that gets me. Usually people are angry before they try to tear your guts out." Mark was gripping the chair arms so violently his knuckles reddened.

"Would you say they know you've exhausted all your resources?"

"They seem to."

"Why would they want you out of business? They may never be paid if you're liquidated." Fred returned to his perch on the desk corner.

"That's what I told the sons-of-bitches." Mark pushed out of the chair and started to pace. "I just can't believe this."

"What do you need short-term, and what do you need long-term to survive the company?" Fred queried casually.

Mark sank back into the chair. "Hell. Short term we need about twenty-five grand; half to pay off one creditor and the balance for one month's operating expenses. He knew the numbers well.

"And long term?" Fred asked impassively.

"Long term we need about half a million dollars to complete the equipment and get to the marketplace." Again Mark shook his head.

"What do you have to offer?"

"In exchange for the short-term money we could offer either bonds, in effect interest bearing promissory notes which I would personally guarantee. Or if I had to, I could give up some company stock." Fred doodled on a scratch pad.

Mark continued. "You once told me not to give up the stock if I believe in it." Fred looked up from the pad.

"I still feel it will be very valuable some day. Besides, I'll probably be forced to give up stock for the long-term money and I don't want to give up control of the company just because of a short-term cash flow problem," Mark finished.

"I'm glad someone listens to me once in awhile," Fred groused. "Excuse me." He went into his private office. Mark thought he heard a metallic clunking noise. A few minutes later Fred returned with a brown paper bag and some business forms.

He sat down in front of Mark and looked at him intently. "Each of us is given at least one second chance in life. You already had yours in Bimini, but you're being given one more."

Curiously Mark eyed the non-descript paper sack.

Fred pulled out a small stack of bills from the bag and counted out twenty-five neat stacks. Fred wrote on the forms and filled in several spaces, then slid the form toward Mark.

"This is an interest bearing promissory note. It is for $25,000 at prime plus one and a half points. I really should charge you prime plus 3 or 4 points since this is speculative, but you've already shown a total personal commitment that convinces me you will make this work. The note is due in two years. You will pay interest only on a quarterly basis. There is no pre-payment penalty. Do you have any questions?"

Mark took the form and carefully read it. Fred smiled. He'd have been very disappointed if Mark had just signed the note.

"There." Mark signed the note. Amazing, he thought. Where did the money come from? Was his friend forgetful in paying Uncle Sam? Anything illicit seemed unlikely. Fred had often cautioned him to be scrupulously honest in all matters.

Deliberately Mark slid the note toward Fred, who accepted

it with only a suggestion of a smile lifting the corners of his mouth. "This is the first, last, and only bail-out I will participate in," said Fred, "since it's against my religion to be a philanthropist. I do not bet on dogs, horses or people." There was no meanness in the way Fred delivered his message. His stern eyes softened as he slid the money across the desk to Mark.

Mark knew that this loan was being given only out of friendship. He was embarrassed that it had been necessary.

"You know I will pay you back no matter what, don't you?" Awkwardly he pocketed the money.

"I have no doubt of it." Fred knew how hard this was for his young friend and did his best not to make Mark any more uncomfortable about it than was absolutely necessary.

"You better get going and put that some place safe." Fred gestured toward the pocket. "Now get out from under my feet. I've a living to make."

Impulsively Mark hugged the older man. "Thanks . . . I . . ."

"Ah Hell, kid, beat it." Fred turned away, quickly easing the door shut. Tears streaked his cheeks.

He'd be paid with interest and had no fear he'd have to write off this loan. It was just a business decision he'd made, he convinced himself.

Quickly Mark strode to the Explorer. He had not dared to hope for such direct assistance. "God grant the opportunity, I'll repay him beyond his dreams." He paused to put on his sunglasses, furtively wiping his eyes.

This was his second promise to the Almighty and he already was in trouble with the first one. He thought of the water, his desperation. And yet in spite of everything, there seemed to be an unalterable direction to his life. Maybe providence did help those who . . .

Watch it, young man. Mark was snapped back to reality as an amply proportioned woman in a Jaguar careened out of the parking lot.

"More money than sense around here," Mark huffed.

CHAPTER FOURTEEN
UP FROM THE DEPTHS

Excitedly, Mark called Linda, but only got her answering machine. "Hi Sugar, it's me, have some good news . . . talk later . . . sorry I missed you." Then he headed for the bank.

"No ma'am," he informed the cashier, "I did not rob a bank, I just like to cause excitement." He was looking forward to stop number three.

"Please tell Mr. Bronson that Mark Hansen would like to see him about his bill." Purposely he didn't reveal the full reason for his call.

"Come in, Mark." The brown-haired man did not stand. He appraised Mark over the rims of his glasses. "I don't want to hurt your feelings but I'm quite busy. If you are here to ask me to back off on the bankruptcy petition, I'm sorry but I just can't do that." Bronson carefully avoided any eye contact.

"Randy, when I first came to see you I told you we were a start-up company. As I recall I also promised you I would pay you." Suspicion, then anxiety crossed Randy's face. "I regret that you lost faith in me." His adversary started to squirm.

"Here is a certified check for everything I owe you. Please mark my account paid in full and notify your attorney you no longer have any cause of action." He looked stone-faced at his former supplier.

Randy stood behind the desk. His pale blue eyes were troubled. "Now Mark, you're taking this personally. I explained to you my reasons." Only the ones I could, he thought angrily.

"You did what you had to do. Now I'll do what I have to do. Good-bye Mr. Bronson." Mark stood and walked rigidly to the door where he paused, turned and said, "My people will pick up my molds next week." He wheeled on one foot and left.

Mark took the receipt to his attorney's office so he could quash the bankruptcy petition. As he sat in the office he reflected upon his good fortune. "Don't get cocky, dude. It was friendship that saved your butt, not smarts."

"Guess what, Joyce?"

"From the look on your face, no more hobo soup?" Joyce asked hopefully.

Mark nodded smugly. "Your paychecks will be good for a while longer."

"My landlady and my grocer thank you." She was relieved. Mark had been candid with her, letting her know the company had financial problems. She was experienced enough to realize not many bosses would take the chance Mark did. There was no way she would let him down by quitting.

Mark went back into the factory and found Daphne working in a corner near the weld-fill machine. She had a hand-pumped hydraulic ram hooked up to a pressure gauge and a one-foot length of steel pipe with screw caps on each end.

"You're gonna love it!" She beamed when he walked up. "Guess what's in the chamber?"

"If it isn't Dom Perignon '57, it should be."

"Close," she grinned, "It's the test sample of the new pressure vessel. If this one is as good as the other two, we're cookin with gas!"

When the gauge hit 18,500 a hissing, gurgling sound erupted from the pipe.

"What the heck is that?"

"Steel just failed. It's okay . . . It held twice as high as the old one." Daphne unscrewed the large retaining cap, then reached in and unscrewed something else. She withdrew a steel pressure vessel that had a torn side.

"Bloody hell." Mark had never seen metal tear. He had seen holes drilled in metal and metal turned and milled, but never torn.

"Damn straight. We done good, Boss. We're back in business."

"I didn't know we were out of business." He was puzzled.

"With all your other worries, I didn't tell you. Augie didn't just incorrectly fabricate equipment. He falsified the burst test data on the pressure vessels. If the Department of Transportation had found out, we wouldn't have been out of business — we'd have been under the jail."

"Dare I ask if there is anything else you have forgotten to mention to me?" Mark stood with both arms across his chest. His pursed lips and raised eyebrows demanded a response.

"No, and it was just dumb luck that I discovered this. I was doing a little quality assurance and the numbers kept coming out wrong. When I checked I found the faked data."

"You are sure it was falsified?" He didn't need to ask. He saw the look. He wondered if Tom had known.

"I double-checked. I even had an outside lab verify the burst strength just to be fair." Daphne brightened. "At least we wound up with a superior vessel. In the long run he accidentally did us a favor."

Mark dropped his arms to his sides. "God knows we need every good break we can get. Speaking of which, Fred loaned us enough to kill the bankruptcy proceeding and keep us afloat a little while longer."

"What? Hey, Mark, did I hear correctly?" Daphne let out a whoop. "Have you told Linda?"

"No, I just left a message on her answering machine."

"This calls for a celebration! You really should take a few days off, Mark. Until we hear on the radar reflectivity tests, there isn't that much that has to be done. Maybe you could take Walt diving in the Keys."

Mark appreciated this little push, since he wanted to go with Walt, but felt guilty about leaving Daphne working in the factory.

"I'm not Malcolm Forbes." She tapped her finger on her forehead, "but even I know Walt has something we need."

"You sure you're not Daphne Forbes?" He gave her a hug, then headed for the door.

Mark glanced through the mail Joyce had left on his desk. A letter from his dad. Slowly he tore open the envelope. A one-page note, enclosing a substantial check. "Even Edison needed help, and I knew you wouldn't ask. Dad." Mark sank into his chair. Hours before he wondered how he would pay his bills, much less afford the diving trip with Walt. Now, unexpectedly from two directions, the help he needed had been provided. Again in disbelief he looked at his father's note. Damn!

Mark confirmed his dive with Walt, agreed to pick him up at his hotel and drive down to Key Largo. He'd called ahead to make arrangements. Since it was mid-week, they were fortunate and were able to obtain a dive boat.

Bogart and Bacall would no longer recognize Key Largo. Now populated by charter boat facilities, modern hotels and motels with both salt and fresh water swimming pools, even a modern medical research facility and diver training schools. The island bore little resemblance to the sparsely populated rural scene of the motion picture.

"So, what camera do you use?" Walt asked as they drove.

"For the wrecks, a Nikonos V, with wide angle 15mm lens. I think I'll use the SB102 Nikonos strobe for close work with a wide angle diffuser."

"Good gear, Mark. What about film?"

"The camera has automatic TTL exposure. So with ultra fine grain film, ISO200 or 400, I can shoot close-ups of props or other features, as well as the larger fish that congregate around the wrecks. It's not the latest technology, but it serves me pretty well."

"Do I understand correctly, the wrecks are both ex-Coast Guard vessels?" Walt looked at the chart.

"Yepper, the Bibb and the Duane. They're both South of

Molasses Reef."

Walt studied the chart.

"If time allows, I'd like to go a little North and film the Christ of the Abyss statue. My lady mentioned she'd like that."

"Sounds good." Mark looked at his ample camera bag. "What equipment are you using?"

"The ships aren't too deep, only about 125 feet I understand, so I thought the Ricoh R-630 camcorder in an underwater Equinox Pro Pack six housing would do." Mark nodded approvingly.

"I brought a wide angle adapter and UR Pro color correction Filter." Mark realized he was no amateur. Like Mark, he had not chosen the latest equipment, but he had chosen well. Mark looked forward to diving with him.

Walt continued. "Look, I know you're certified, but I've heard there's a medical research firm working with a private company here that offers instruction and training in Nitrox dives."

Mark chimed in, "So we could dive deeper, longer . . ."

"Just so." Walt confirmed. "Let's check it out."

"You'll be able to double your diving time on the bottom, without need for decompression," Anders told them. "We furnish the equipment and five hours of instruction, including classroom, pool and then a confirmation ocean dive."

"Works for me." Mark liked the idea."Let's do it tomorrow morning." Walt turned to Anders. "May we dive on the wreck of the Bibb in the afternoon as our ocean dive?"

"Sure. That's a standard dive. You'll be able to spend nearly 40 minutes on the bottom, without decompression." He checked his schedule book. "That's confirmed for tomorrow, gentlemen."

"If we're going to work the cameras tomorrow, maybe we should check out the photo lab today."

"Good idea. There's a dynamite photographic lab just a few hundred feet down US 1 from the motel. Let's check it out."

"I've dived all over the world, from Fiji to the Med, but I've never found a location with better facilities for underwater photographers." Walt bought several lenses and some fittings.

After dinner the two men walked down to a large coral rock building that was decorated with natural wood. They'd decided to wa!k off an over-ample dinner.

"Stop for a drink?"

"Just one. Then it's sack time."

The band was playing top 40 music. Mark was glad they were only staying for one drink.

"Perrier with a twist," Mark told the waiter.

"Evian and a twist," Walt added.

"Don't dive and drink," Mark smiled as he paraphrased.

"Just so," the visitor acknowledged.

"The other day you mentioned an interest in mariculture. What direction is that taking in Japan?"

"You are truly interested?"

"I am."

"Multi-cropping of different species of aquatic animals and plants together seems to hold much promise. We are hopeful that . . ."

Mark listened intently and the evening passed quickly.

The following morning they attended class and in the afternoon they headed to the site of the wreck of the Bibb.

"There's just something about these older wooden boats." Admiringly Mark appraised the dive boat. She was about 60-feet long and well laid out. There were racks for the scuba tanks, and all necessary facilities for the comfort and safety of the divers.

"Yes." Walt relaxed against the polished rail. "There is a character and feel that just isn't captured in fiberglass or aluminum." Idly he rubbed the bright work.

"What do you think, fellows?" Anders sauntered up to Mark and propped a foot on the bottom rail.

"Looking good," Mark offered. "Seas about three feet?"

Anders nodded agreement. "Time to saddle up."

Mark looked over the side. The sea was as clear as the sparkling waters they drank the evening before. Anders helped Mark with his gear. He secured something to his harness that looked like a flashlight.

"This is a Screamer. It's an underwater emergency alarm."

He held it in front of Mark. "In quiet-one mode it's a signal, just to attract the attention of a fellow diver. In alarm-two it sends the emergency distress signal. You can hear it several hundred yards away."

He triggered the alarm, nearly shattering Mark's eardrum. "See!"

Mark wasn't thrilled.

"Here. One more thing. Put this on your wrist. It's a Suunto ML dive computer. Remember to keep track of time and depth. It'll keep you alive and me out of trouble."

"Gentlemen, the Bibb is lying on her side. She had a forty-foot beam, so the top rail is only ninety feet below the surface." Anders walked from diver to diver, triple checking their equipment. "Let's make this a safe dive. My boss gets very upset if I don't bring everyone back."

Mark wondered if Anders knew about his problem in the Bahamas or if this was just a chance remark. He said nothing; his mouth was too dry anyway.

Walt cleared his mask and looked at the ship's rail. "Mariko will love this."

"Large fish are abundant, and the details of the ship are easy to see and film. Have fun." Anders went over the stern.

"Perfecto," Mark exclaimed to himself. "Perfect for a mixed gas dive, perfect for photography as well." He checked his dive computer. They had agreed to limit bottom time to thirty minutes.

"Watch out for time dilation," they were warned. "Time speeds up on a deep dive, so pay attention to your dive computers, your instructors and your dive partners."

Mark recalled that Walt particularly wanted to film the wheelhouse and any debris surrounding the wreck. Think I'll film Walt filming the wreck, he decided. It would make a nice gift for Mariko.

They grouped near the stern of the dive boat and then, as a unit, headed slowly down toward the ship's rail dimly gleaming in the depths. Mark, Walt and Anders tended to cluster as they roamed the bottom, photographing the Bibb.

Mark started to film Walt, who was intent on detailing the ship's wheel. He lost sight of him as he swam behind the housing.

"Weeeeeeooooooo . . ." Abruptly, he heard and felt a piercing noise. His dive computer showed twenty-five minutes on the bottom.

"What the hell is that?" He dropped his camera, which slowly drifted up toward the surface. Frantically he searched for the source of the noise.

A Screamer alarm was sounding. "Oh crap, where's Walt?" Immediately he checked, finding him all right, then he checked for Anders. Dimly, toward the bow he made out the instructor, giving a visual distress signal.

"Remind me never to dive again," Mark scolded him. He struggled against the current to reach the other diver. Chills tingled his fingers and toes.

He handed the buddy breathing hose to Anders, who quickly stuck it in his mouth and gulped down the saving air. *Why me?* he was thinking, as he prepared to alternate breathing with the distressed diver. Cramps pierced his shoulder and neck muscles.

As he looked into Anders' mask and searched his eyes, Mark quickly realized there was no emergency. The Instructor was testing him.

"Son-of-a-bitch. No one said anything about this during the class instruction." As he took back his hose, Anders gave him the thumbs up sign and a reassuring rub on the forearm. "Hell, they're right, I guess. Better to find out with the Instructor than to have an accident later."

Walt, who had arranged the whole thing, smiled to himself as he watched the "rescue." Someday his friend would enjoy watching the video shots of the entire drama. Mark was not the only one documenting the dive for a friend's loved one. Walt knew that Linda would treasure the video.

Mark pointed upward and signaled he was going to retrieve his camera, which by now was well on its way to the surface. Walt nodded and the three divers linked on a gradual assent.

Back on the surface, the divers were greeted with warm mugs of coffee. “Thanks, you're a life saver,” Mark shivered slightly as he shed his gear.

“Cold?” asked Walt.

“Memories of things past.” he answered truthfully.

“Understood.” Walt nodded.

“Mark, I do not wish to be rude by bringing up business at such a time, but I have thought about your Locator since Sean first described it to me.” He paused thoughtfully.

“As you must realize, there is great difficulty in bringing American-made products into Japan. Every pretext is used to keep foreign products out.”

“So I'm told.”

“Still, it may be that some people I know,” he avoided the use of the word “partners,” “. . . might be interested in distribution of such a product and might assist in securing needed approvals.”

“That would be appreciated.” Mark smiled. “We would be
pleased to express our gratitude in an appropriate and traditional manner.”

“You have developed an appreciation of Asian ways, I see.”

“One tries.” He bowed slightly.

“If you will pardon one more impertinence, I understand that before you need a distributor, you need an investor.”

“Just so.” He borrowed an expression and returned it.

“Paul mentioned to you a rather unusual gentleman from New Zealand, I believe.”

Mark looked quizzically at his friend. He wondered where the conversation was leading. How did he know?

“It so happens that I sent the man to Paul. Also, it so happens that the man is in West Palm Beach now. With your agreement I would like to get you two together.”

“It so happens,” grinned Mark, “that I would like that just fine. He could visit the plant. Could you tell me a little about him?”

"A little. His name is Abraham Steinmetz." Seeing the surprise in Mark's eyes, he continued, "Yes, a Jewish Kiwi."

"How is it that . . .?"

"Ahh . . . you see," Walt continued, "Japan has nothing to fear from such a tiny country . . . rich in natural resources. There are many wealthy and influential Jews there. Our interests . . ."

"Whatever it takes." Mark nodded.

"Just so." Walt grinned.

"Personally, what sort of man is this Abraham?"

"A friend."

"Just so." Mark grinned.

"One other thing." The casual way it was mentioned told Mark just how important it would be.

"Yes."

"He too shares an interest in science, in radioactivity to be more specific."

"Most unusual," Mark replied, "his country is very anti-nuclear."

"You will find he is a very unusual man."

"Just so." Mark smiled.

CHAPTER FIFTEEN
TESTING

A blue jay and a mockingbird were quarreling over breadcrumbs in the early morning sunlight when Abraham and Walt arrived at the plant. Dodging the battling birds, Mark ushered the guests into the reception area.

The New Zealander wasn't at all what Mark expected. Actually he was not sure what he expected.

Abraham gave Mark's hand a vigorous shake. Vigorous hell. He nearly broke it. Mark never flinched, but Abraham read his expression. "No flabby Miami Beach Jew, eh." he grinned.

Mark flushed, uncertain about how to respond.

"Your reaction is most natural." Abraham placed a brotherly hand on the younger man's shoulder. "My build and color throw off many people." Pausing, he added. "Who's your lovely companion?"

"Daphne Leyland, I'd like you to meet Abraham Steinmetz."

Daphne extended her hand. "How do you do."

"I do very well, thank you." Abraham smiled warmly, his eyes doing a quick appraisal. "So you're the engineer I've been hearing about."

"You're from New Zealand, Mr. . . . "

"Please, my dear, call me Abraham." He waved a ringed finger in the air as if to dismiss all formality. "Yes, but only indirectly. After the War my family lived in Israel and then in Auckland . . . and here I am."

"You are indeed," thought Daphne. He was only slightly shorter than Mark, and appeared nearly as fit.

"I like Florida," he continued, escorting her to a chair. "Weather, sports. I enjoy tennis and back home we play cricket." He grinned, patting his muscular belly. "It does help keep the flab away." Abruptly he turned to Mark. "Now, if you'll pardon my further bluntness, I understand from Walt that you have a product with a lot of potential, but you need money to tool up your plant and you need distributors internationally. Is that about right?"

Walt seemed to blend in to the furniture, an enigmatic smile tracing his lips.

"Well . . . Yes . . . that's about right." Mark was caught short by the sharply contrasting styles of Walt and Abraham. Quickly he regained his composure. "We're finally on track with the product. Thanks to Daphne." Glancing in her direction, he then continued. "There were quite a few development glitches we were fighting. Now we're tooling the plant. We need money and we need distribution. In that order."

Abraham frowned and eyed him intently. "Do you have a patent and do you have financials?"

"No and yes. A U. S. patent is applied for, and as soon as we have some cash we'll apply in Europe, Japan and Australia. I have a current balance sheet and complete financials are available."

"O.K., I'll want to fax any information to my barrister in Auckland and my accountant will need a look. In the meantime, I'd like to see the product demonstrated." From his shirt pocket he removed bifocal halfies, and with a practiced eye studied the patent drawing Mark handed him. Satisfied, he smiled at Mark and Daphne. "I'm making no promises, but your product appears to fill a need somewhat peculiar to my part of the world."

"Walt tells me you have no paid professional Coast

Guard." Mark probed; assuring himself that he understood the need Abe referred to.

"He's correct. In fact, even though Australia has a population of many times that of ours, about 18 million people, they don't have a paid professional Coast Guard either."

"Darn. That must make survival a big problem." He thought of his own close call. Muscles in his neck tightened.

"Remember Mark, our water is colder than yours. Like Alaska. You don't last long in 40 degree water."

"I wasn't doing that well in 60 degree water."

Again Abraham eyed Mark intently. "I heard about your near miss. But you realize also our winds are stronger than yours, waves higher. If it works, a product like yours would be even more valuable to us than to you."

"Then you would have an interest if I can prove to you the product works?" Mark's eyes brightened.

"I would of course want exclusivity as distributor for New Zealand, possibly for Australia as well." Abraham put up one finger solemnly. "As you say, that's contingent upon the suitability of your product, and your ability to produce. Naturally." Keenly he appraised Mark over the tops of bifocals.

"If we can structure something that's mutually profitable, I would like that very much." Mark responded directly. "What do you think would be a valid test of the product?"

"No lab bullshit. Let's take my boat, go offshore a few miles from Pompano and field-test some units."

Daphne leaned forward. "If I may interrupt just a second. What type of boat and what type of radar?"

"Fifty-foot Lauderdale with 25 mile range Furuno radar. All right?"

"Fine." She nodded.

"Perfect," Mark seconded. "How about we put six units out on life jackets, run off 15 or 20 miles and then try to find them. Would you accept that as a valid demonstration?"

"If five of the six are found, that would be acceptable. Subject to that, I'd be interested in a deal."

"Why don't you bring your engineer along." He waved in

Daphne's direction. "Since I'll have a lady friend with me."

"If you don't mind, I'll bring my fiancée Linda, and Daphne could bring her friend."

"Agreed." He rose, moved over and held Daphne's hand. "We'll look forward to a successful demonstration on Sunday."

Walt escorted him to the door. "See you in Auckland, Abraham."

Mark was startled. "You'll not be joining us?"

A slight upturn at the corners of his mouth gave away Walt's pleasure. "Not this time. My work here is completed." Slowly he raised his right hand to firmly grasp Mark's. "See you in Auckland."

The door swung shut before Mark could clarify the statement. He stared at the door.

"They do love their mystery, don't they?" Daphne remarked lightly.

"I hope you brought plenty of sunscreen. Look at that sky." Mark shielded his eyes and gazed out over the water.

A flock of seagulls cruised past on their way from the shore to the landfills where they found free meals and warmth. The incinerator's plume of smoke must have served as a lighthouse, a beacon for the birds to home on. Mark found it strange they would prefer that environment to their home, the ocean.

"Couldn't have picked a better day for a radar test." Linda beamed. "Just a hint of a breeze to take the edge off the heat."

"Wait till you see the ship." Mark hurried her toward the dock's end.

Barbara had already informed Linda the main salon was air-conditioned and had a color TV, wet bar and stereo.

"Lollypop! I love that name," she exclaimed as they approached the ship. "Oh my gosh. It's lovely."

"She's as tough as she's fashionable." A voice drifted down from the tuna tower. Abraham leaned over and waved them aboard. From the tower he could see clearly in all directions.

"Well, it's perfect for testing." Mark looked up at the radar scanner with great satisfaction.

"As you see, we have dual controls for the motors and steering located in the tower. Andy, the captain, prefers to run from here, especially for fishing." Abraham slid down the ladder and extended a hand to Linda. "Welcome aboard. I understand you're to be congratulated."

Linda blushed. "Thank you." At once she felt comfortable with Abraham. Mark was right. He was a find. Now, if only . . .

Mark was smiling at her, and for a moment their eyes met.

"Ah, there's Daphne and her friend." Abraham shifted to the stern. "We're all here. Let's get going."

"Hi everyone." Daphne leaped the transom, landing gracefully on the afterdeck. Her male friend stumbled over the rail and awkwardly situated himself by the fishing chair. "Mark, Abraham, this is Peter Warden."

"Hello Madam Engineer, ready for the test?" Abraham warmly greeted her.

"You bet." Daphne looked over the ship and grinned. Good day. Good ship. Good people . . . we'll see. For her there was another test besides the product test going on that day. Her feelings toward Peter were also being tested. After that surprise walk-in, she wondered if she really could forget what he'd done—she wondered if there had been others.

"Sondra." Abraham called to his friend. "Our guests have arrived." A short dark-haired woman appeared by the salon door.

"Daphne, Peter, Linda, Mark, I'd like you to meet my friend Sondra Walsh."

Linda was immediately struck by Sondra's beauty. Her skin was pale, a strong contrast to Abe's. As she moved closer a pair of lovely brown eyes warmly greeted them.

"I'm so pleased to meet you." Sondra smiled graciously.

"Please, let's get comfortable in the salon." She motioned toward the door. "Its already cooled down inside."

They left the dock at 11:00 in order to catch the high tide

through the pass to the ocean. The Lollypop pounded through the channel.

Mark frowned, a worried crease appearing on his brow. Perceiving his anxiety, Linda came over to him. "Are you O.K. honey?"

"What?" He was listening to one engine on the ship that was running a little rough. With every vibration and missed beat, his stomach knotted.

Gently she rubbed his forearm and the knots loosened. "I'm all right. Just a little tense I guess." What the hell, he added to himself, just our whole future rests on six temperamental Locators.

Mark and Abe moved to the tower above the salon, to lay out the test.

"Daphne, if you don't mind I'd like to go back on deck." Peter lifted his fingers, waving to her. "I'd like to sample the ocean air."

"Oh — Peter, are you sure?" Daphne called after him. "Wouldn't you like to stay inside a little longer?" She tried to hide her disappointment. She'd so hoped everyone would accept him. She'd so hoped—

"Sorry everyone, but I think I'd feel better outside in the fresh air." Peter smiled sheepishly, his fingers still fluttering behind him in mid-air as he turned his back on the party and headed for the transom.

Daphne ran after him and tugged him by the arm. "Peter, maybe you'll feel better if you have some soda. I'll get us some." She returned to the salon. "I'm sorry we're not good company today. Maybe some soda will help."

Linda smiled sympathetically and gave her friend a hug. "Don't worry, we understand. Here, take something to eat too." She pulled out a packet of crackers.

Two hours later Mark stood at the lee side of the tuna tower with a Locator poised for firing. Abraham looked on approvingly.

"C'mon baby, fill up and fly." Fly baby fly, he prayed to himself. This was the sixth unit. It was well past noon and Mark had already fired and flawlessly deployed five units. Dropped randomly at two-mile intervals, the Locators were soaring in the bright Gulfstream sun. As the sixth balloon raced upward, he shouted. "Go, you bitch."

Mark slumped against the tower railing, every muscle in his body going limp. It was working! The last balloon continued to rise.

"If it's O.K. with you, we'll take a curving path away from the cluster of sample units and then reverse course and try to find them," Abraham suggested.

"Yes, that's good. They're like a boat crew scattered on the ocean after a sea disaster." Yeah, he repeated, a cold shiver passing through him. He wondered if one ever forgot a near-death escape.

He thought about a real search. The ship would not already know the location of the survivors. Did he dare up the ante? Daphne noticed the muscles tightening at the base of his jaw. What could he be thinking of?

"Let's turn the radar down during the trip away from the balloons, then power up after we're 15 or 20 miles away from the last drop point," Mark snapped.

"Very good Mark," Abe agreed, "That makes an even more realistic test of how the product would be expected to operate." Pausing, he first looked at the radar, then glanced back at Mark and Daphne. "Let it all hang out, eh." He chuckled.

"Notify us when we're at least 15 miles from the balloons," he yelled to Andy, then motioning to Mark and Daphne. "Let's join the party in the salon."

Linda and Sondra were deep in conversation. "Guess what Mark," Linda exclaimed, "Sondra is from Coral Gables," smiling conspiratorially, "and she knows Gene Meson, you remember Sean's favorite artist. He shows at a friend's gallery."

"Ah, yes." Mark grinned at the two of them. Linda was a remarkable person. She seemed to be able to find a common bond with almost anyone.

Mark couldn't fault Abe's taste in women. Wide-set eyes accented her delicate features. She moved with the power and grace of a tennis player. Mark hoped he'd get to know both Abraham and Sondra better. It would be a nice foursome. And Abraham—if everything worked out—he looked past the stern.

"Would you'all excuse me," Mark motioned toward Peter on the afterdeck, "I'm going to see how he's doing."

While Abe jumped into the conversation, Mark joined Peter, who he felt was not a bad sort, though maybe a little flabby.

"How's it going, mate?" He sat down in a fishing chair.

"Not too well, a little sea-sick, I think."

"How about a motion sickness pill?" Mark offered. "Or better yet, a beer?"

"Thanks." Peter nodded glumly. For a while the two men sipped their beers and watched as the shore receded into the dividing line between land and sky. Only the plumes from the incinerator and the power plant muddied the clear blue sky.

"15 miles," the captain yelled before Mark had finished his second Corona.

"Want to come up and watch the recoveries?" Mark asked.

"Thanks for the invite, but I think I'll stay here."

"All right." Turning to the bridge, Abe yelled, "O.K. Cap, please power up the radar. Let's go hunting."

"O.K. See you up top." Mark climbed the ladder to the bridge. He felt sorry for Peter. "Not a bad sort, just out of his element," he thought.

Abraham was already there when Mark arrived, Daphne with him. Linda and Sondra elected to stay in the comfort of the salon.

Linda leaned out of the salon. "Peter do you want to join us?" Reluctantly he accepted. The afterdeck was taking some sea spray because of the change in course of the ship, so he welcomed the invitation to get out of the weather. "It's getting a bit dark and nasty out there."

"Son-of-a-bitch, I see seven or eight blips," Abraham was already excitedly looking at the radarscope. "Unless those are all yachts, we have a good return from the balloons. Look at that!"

"Theory is, the balloons show up like 30-to-40 foot yachts on radar." Mark tried his best to act matter-of-fact as he responded.

"Andy, let's make speed toward the nearest blip." Through the binoculars Abraham scanned the air for a balloon. He searched the azimuth indicated from the radar.

"Thar she blows!" Radar showed the target to be about five miles away. Abraham sighted a balloon.

"Look at that. I can see it now," Daphne yelled. Without binoculars they saw the balloon three miles away. It glistened in the sun like a polished mirror.

"That's one," Mark said.

They continued. Shortly Daphne yelled, "Look, over there."

"That's two." He grinned. The boat surged ahead.

"Three," he shouted excitedly a few moments later. Waves pounded. Skies darkened. Diesel fumes drifted past as they slowed to recover another balloon.

Then they sighted number four. Mark's heart pounded. Would they find one more? Would they have found Mark if he were in the water?

"Are we having fun yet, Boss?" Daphne moved to his side.

"Do da sea have salt?" He laughed aloud, his teeth chattering as a chill swept him.

"Pretty neat, sir," the captain volunteered.

"Do they work in the rain?" Abraham addressed Mark.

"They better." He grinned.

"Sir." The captain was pointing off the bow.

"That's five." Daphne pressed against his arm. Mark could feel her trembling. It was too good to be true.

Abraham grabbed Mark by the shoulder and steered him to one side of the bridge. "I've looked at your numbers and so has my barrister and my accountant. I'll give you $650,000 for 45% of the company and I also get exclusive distribution rights for the Pacific Rim, including New Zealand and Australia. I don't get Japan, because I think that would be unfair to Walt. I think he should get that for putting us together."

Mark swallowed and took a deep breath, controlling his excitement. He was tempted to leap at the offer, but he paid attention to what Sean and Fred had told him. He smiled at Abe and countered, "Make that $650,000 for 30% of the company with an option for another 10% at $300,000 and we have a deal."

Without releasing his grip on Mark's shoulder, Abe returned, "$650,000 for 35% and $200,000 for another 10%, plus distribution is included."

Mark half-turned to Abe and said, "$650,000 for 30% and the option of $250,000 for another 10% and you get Pacific Rim, less Japan, which Walt gets, if he makes a reasonable distribution deal with me. Naturally you'll have a seat on the Board of Directors of the company."

Both men, grinning broadly, had already started to extend their hands.

It was only a good deal, if it was a good deal for everyone, thought Mark, and this was fair all the way around.

Abe and Mark swung toward Daphne. Tom Sawyer and Huckleberry Finn, she thought with humor.

"Meet our new corporate partner," Mark announced.

Daphne hugged both men. Tears flowed down her cheeks.

The Captain looked over his shoulder and said, "So when can I have one of those puppies?" They had a winner.

Mark, Abe and Daphne plunged down the ladder to the salon. Linda watched as they slammed through the door together.

Their victory was obvious. Wordlessly, Linda hugged each of them. When Abraham broke the news about their partnership, she was speechless.

Mark picked up Linda and swung her around. Then he did the same with Daphne. Abraham followed suit with Sondra.

"This is so great," Sondra enthused to Linda. "He hasn't been this excited since he got the big boat in New Zealand." She didn't know the exact numbers involved, but she knew that Abe had spent over four million for his floating palace as she called it.

"Big boat?" Linda's eyes widened.

"Isn't this awesome?" Glowed Daphne, giving Linda a bearhug.

"Oh Daphne it wouldn't have happened without you." Linda hugged her in return.

Daphne grinned bashfully. "Thank you Lord!" She prayed silently. She knew how lucky they'd been. So lucky that Linda . . . what . . .? Her friend was trying to tell her something. That look . . . She knew.

"Son-of-a-bitch." She wished she didn't know. What had Peter . . .

She pulled Linda aside. "Sondra?" asked Daphne.

Linda nodded. "He came up behind her as she poured a drink, and ran his hand down her back . . . way down her back . . . in front of me. Really dumb. But Sondra was terrific. She handled him well." Daphne stiffened.

"Damn." she fumed. "I should've known." She stalked over to Sondra, making sure that Peter was within hearing range.

"Sondra, if my guest caused you any discomfort, I'd like to apologize to you on his behalf."

She turned to Peter. "I thought you were a little smarter, making such an ass of yourself. You can drive home alone. Mark and Linda, if it's all right, I'll go home with you."

"Daphne, honey," Peter whined. "What's the matter with you people? Don't you have a sense of humor?" He eased toward Daphne. "I didn't mean anything."

"Forget it Peter," Mark said mildly. "No one's going to let your petty bullshit spoil this day." Inwardly he was relieved the little incident had occurred. Painful as it was for her, Daphne at last would see what kind of person she was involved with. Now it would be easier for her to shed him.

"So, madam engineer . . . What do we need to do next?" Abraham came up to them.

"Get to the market promptly," Daphne directed. "Right after the party!"

CHAPTER SIXTEEN
DARK CLOUDS

"Sugar, those scowl lines are going to ruin that handsome face," Linda began, "what's so important?"

"Oh, just thinking how lucky we've been." He pulled her closer to him on the bed. "Fred told me most start-ups expire before they even get this far. The Pacific Rim should generate enough orders at least temporarily to solve the marketing problem. We have ample capital, barring a major calamity, to fund the company until it's self-sustaining. Thanks to you, we have Daphne's able assistance in the plant."

"Aren't you being a little too modest?"

"Honey, I have no illusions about my business skill or ability. We are where we are because we're too bull-headed to quit and because we have loyal friends."

Gently he turned her head toward him and gave her a tender kiss.

"Mark, you're hopeless. No one else could have done what you've done so far."

"I'm not sure of that. But it seems to me I owe a lot to some good friends, and somehow I'm going to repay them. Anyway, I think we're all part of something bigger we may never understand. Maybe we should just relax and enjoy it."

"At last we agree. Come here." She pulled him closer.

"There's one thing bugging me. That guy named Adams." Mark scowled. "You know, the one from American Entertainment Corporation. He's supposedly an acquisitions specialist, but seems to be, well slimey." He sat up.

Realizing he had broken the mood, he scooted down beside her again. "Sorry honey. I didn't mean for business to intrude on us." Stroking her hair, he explained, "It's just that I have a bad feeling about this guy. Why would an entertainment firm want to buy Locator? Besides, he looks and acts like, well a pimp."

"Didn't you have Ordean or Fred check him out?"

"Yes. The company has plenty of bucks. But no one seems to know anything about them. Fred's still checking."

"So what's this Adams person like?"

"He's an average looking guy, about five nine, maybe about 160 lbs. Not fat, but not fit. Not suntanned and yet he didn't have that Yankee pallor." Mark paused, trying to evaluate what he remembered. His speech sounded like native Dade County, a mix of Ohio Midwestern overtones layered on Georgia or Alabama southern.

"What does he wear?"

"Ahh . . . A suit that was tailored but gaudy. He carried a black leather briefcase. Very sturdy . . . usually I'd have thought nothing of it. Yet it seemed, well . . . out of place."

"How did you meet him?"

"Out of the blue his secretary called to make an appointment. Very professional though. But when I told him we weren't interested in selling, his reaction was strange. He couldn't believe it. When he came back today he was even stranger."

Again the scene replayed. Adams addressed Mark:

"My people are naturally very disappointed that you lack interest in what they feel is a more than generous offer for your shares in Locator. A half a million is a lot of money." Adams inhaled deeply, slowly rotating a pencil around in his hand. "You strike me as a fair-minded man. Since my people feel their offer constitutes a good deal, they're wondering what they could do to persuade you that the offer is good for you. They're not unreasonable." He paused hopefully.

Mark casually looked at his fingernails.

"How would you like to see this offer changed to alter your perception so that you might view it favorably?" It flowed out almost as if it had been memorized. As he spoke, Adams had focused his eyes on the picture behind Mark. It was a photo of Linda. He continued to avoid contact with Mark's eyes.

Mark was annoyed. This guy would be more at home in a pink caddy, sipping a Grasshopper and talking to his pink poodle, he thought to himself. Even so, it would be unwise to underestimate him. Fred once told Mark that a false sense of security may set a person up for the big kill.

The word "kill" echoed in his ear. Adams was saying, "We're not just killing time here." He shuffled his feet self-consciously and dropped the pencil onto the desk. "Don't you think you had better rethink this?"

"Possibly so. I have no plans to sell my interest in Locator, but I'm a businessman and I'd like to think I'm willing to look at an offer with an open mind. I'd like to think your principals would consider some sort of a reasonable counter offer with equally open minds."

Adams realized he was being dismissed, but that another meeting was almost certain. At least it's not a flat-out rejection like the first time, he thought, fearing what his boss would say.

Possibly he'd been a little heavy-handed, thinking that Mark must certainly know who he represented. Maybe this man was as green and innocent as he appeared. Or maybe he was a snake cleverly hiding beneath some twigs.

Hermine had warned him, "Watch the twigs, some day one may be a viper." Since then he watched where he walked and where he stuck his hand in the business jungle. He accepted his dismissal with a courteous handshake.

"Maybe we can meet again at your convenience, possibly next week?" Mark shook his head and nodded curtly. Nevertheless, Adams was optimistic when he left the office.

As the image faded, Mark rolled over on his side, tapping thoughtfully on Linda's arm. "This is like landing in Oz. First we're broke, now we've got two offers for the company. Everyone loves a winner."

"Gee whiz, what happened to Mr. Modest?"

"Come on, you know what I mean. When you're down you find out who your real friends are. When you're up, everyone wants to be your friend." He stretched out full length on the bed and breathed deeply.

"How's this?" Linda kneaded his tense shoulder muscles."Terrible. Why don't you keep it up until you get it right?" She smacked him.

"You are such a waste. Do you know what any other sane man would give to be in your place right now?" Roughly she shook him.

"In your bed?"

"No dammit. Well . . . Yes that too."

"You're right, sugar. But it is our future."

Linda realized how worried he really was. Amazing, she thought. Just when things look like they're all working out . . .

"I'm not impressed with the Taiwan offer," Mark said. "Abraham thinks they don't have the financial horsepower to really do anything with the company. Daphne said they had no natural source of helium and had to import it from Belgium or the United States. She thinks they're just after a leveraged buyout to get a helium supply and gain access to the U. S. markets."

"Daphne knew all that." Linda said with new respect. "Aren't you glad I got you all together?"

"Yes she did, and yes I am."

"Do we know who's behind the Taiwan company?"

"No, but I have my suspicions. Tom still has a non-compete agreement." He reflected on the irony of his situation. "Anyway these guys are legitimate businessmen and they had good reputations in world trade. I wouldn't arbitrarily close the door on them."

"So have you decided how to handle this man Adams?"

"Abraham suggested we let him stew for a week. Then we inform him we feel a fair price for the company would be two million dollars, based not on assets or book value, but on the net present value of the income stream the company would produce for the next ten years."

Linda shook her head incredulously. "My God, sugar, is it really worth that?"

"Yeah, we really think so." The thought even impressed Mark.

A week later he met with Adams again. Upon hearing the value Mark placed on the company, his jaw dropped and his beady eyes drew together angrily. Quickly he regained his composure.

"Are you nuts?" He smiled benignly. "The company is not worth that much. If you're smart you'll put a more realistic price on it, or better yet accept our first offer."

Mark chose silence.

"Look Mark, you're young and in good health, you have a young and healthy girlfriend, maybe you'd be better staying that way and enjoying the money from the company rather than risking the uncertainties that the future holds for all of us."

Mark slowly rose to his feet, easing his chair back against the wall. "Mr. Adams, you may leave now."

Mark crashed down in his chair and ran a hand over his eyes. "I should've broken the little dip's neck," he muttered. His heart pounded. Just when everything was going right.

Later that day Mark received a call from the secretary for the Treasurer of the American Entertainment Corporation. "Mr. Trope wants to apologize for any misunderstanding and he'd like you to be his guest for lunch. Please accept his invitation. He really would like an opportunity to talk to you."

Reluctantly Mark agreed to an informal meeting at Skin Dancers the following Wednesday afternoon. At least it would give him a chance to tell them what he thought of the little bastard Adams.

Mark set up a meeting with Sean at the hobby shop later that day. At Mark's request, Sean and Fred had been asking around about the American Entertainment and about Trope and Adams.

Sean looked grim as the tall man approached his desk.

"Well Mark, you were right. These guys are bad actors. The word on the street says these folks are from the northeast and are connected with the mob. They're trying to move in on legitimate businesses. They have a lot of cash and are trying to hide the money."

"Lovely. Now I've got the Mafia up my ass."

"Not exactly. The thing of it is, apparently they're not Mafia connected. Even the mob has some ethics when it comes to kiddie porn."

"Get real. What the hell would porno creeps want with an emergency locator?"

"This guy Trope owns a string of titty bars and bookstores. You know books, plastic toys and peep shows. He started outside Chicago and then came down here. He hooked in with the white slavers in Colombia and Russia. Now he has it all, dope – girls . . . Supposedly they even do snuff films."

Mark shivered.

"What about the creep that came to see me—Adams?"

"Adams used to be a flunky in a credit analysis department of a bank until he married Trope's sister. He's little more than a lap dog for Trope. But don't let that fool you. Supposedly Adams had been the trigger man for at least two killings."

"Killings?"

"One, a girl who was working as a bit player in skin flicks, got caught dealing drugs for Trope. They don't appreciate private enterprise. Worse, the girl was going to talk to a grand jury. She wound up in the trunk of a car at the Lauderdale airport." Mark's stomach turned over. A cold lump rose in the back of his throat.

"Another," Sean went on, "a guy who ran a fiberglass boat building company near Naples, Florida. Seems the boys wanted his business and he didn't want to sell, so he wound up sleeping with the groupers. Looked like an accident, he'd been drinking and drowned while fishing off a boat near Everglades City. Funny thing, he was diabetic and didn't drink."

"Nice people."

"Anyway, nothing has been pinned on them. It's your bad luck if you fit their want list perfectly."

"Want list?"

"They're looking for legitimate businesses, preferably in import-export with good growth potential. You're perfect — you'll need expansion capital to grow."

"How the hell did you find out all this crap?" Visibly shaken, Mark sank into a chair, running a hand over his damp forehead.

"Remember Lt. Lopez? He owed me one. And besides, he'd like to get these guys. They've made the sheriff look like a real putz in court twice. The department wants 'em bad. They used to stick to cash businesses like titty bars and strip joints and such, but those are too obvious and are being watched too closely. Their organization doesn't need that kind of attention."

"Lucky us."

"There's one other thing," said Sean. "The word is that these guys are well connected politically. They own some senators, judges and military personnel already. You know money talks and bullshit walks."

Mark shook his head and swore under his breath. Wearily he rubbed his eyes and peered through his fingers at Sean.

"So how do they operate?"

"Normally what they do is just try to buy the company cheap. If that doesn't work, they try to lend the company more money than it can handle."

Many strange events of late suddenly made sense. "So if they can engineer financial mistakes and get you in over your head, then they wind up in control that way. If that doesn't work, they resort to friendly persuasion. If that doesn't work they resort to unfriendly persuasion."

Sean eased back in his chair. The two men exchanged hard looks. "I know that isn't good news, but that's what I hear anyway."

"Thanks, I think."

"At the risk of sounding melodramatic, if they make a reasonable offer or even an almost reasonable offer, you might be wise to accept it. Cash out and go clip coupons or whatever."

Mark stood up and started to pace the floor. "Never happen." He shook his fist. "And see them destroy what we built?" He shook his head. "No way."

Sean's eyes trailed after his friend as he continued to pace. He wondered if Mark understood how dangerous Adams and company really were. "From what I gather, they don't go in and pillage and plunder a company like some corporate raiders. Quite the opposite. It's in their interest to see the company prosper and grow legitimately." If somehow he could persuade Mark to get out gracefully.

"Sons of bitches," Mark growled.

"You might negotiate golden parachutes for you and Daphne, so you're taken care of. What the hell, not only would you get out clean financially, but you'd wind up with a good consulting contract. They built a big chain of video stores and sold out to a legit national entertainment company in Fort Lauderdale. Now they have tons of cash and are looking for a home."

"Fat chance," muttered Mark.

"Really, it might not be a bad deal for you after all. Frankly I think you'll be safer and more secure financially than if you tried to slug it out with them."

"Screw that." Mark rubbed his neck. "It isn't the American way even if it makes sense."

He stopped pacing and glanced sideways at Sean. "The idea of turning my company over to porno punks, sucks. Skin flicks are one thing, but kids . . . Why don't we just give them the whole damn country and move to Benwabi to start all over from scratch?"

Sean fell silent, gazing down at his hands. Ideals, he thought bitterly, where do they lead? Wasn't that what Nam had been about? At least Desert Storm was some vindication. Still . . .

"Mark, I admire your attitude," he said finally, "but I question your judgment."

"If you'll pardon my saying so, a guy with three purple hearts doesn't sound too swift trying to tell someone else about playing it safe," Mark chided, coming over and laying a hand on his shoulder.

"Well . . ." Again their eyes met. "Aw, hell." Sean grinned

anxiously.

"Before I make up my mind, I'll talk to Fred. I'll see you later." Mark paused at the stairs. "And thanks, really. I appreciate the concern."

Mark started down the stairs and again paused. "Oh, before I forget. Remember last month we were talking about photo-voltaic cells?"

"Yeah."

"You said no electric power would be generated from an X-ray striking the cell, but it would destroy the cell eventually."

Sean rose and moved over to the stair well. "Yeah."

"What would happen if I put a screen, like a conditioner or a converter between the X-ray and the photo-voltaic cell?"

Although the question had been posed casually, Sean realized immediately the depth of thought process behind it. Laughing, he replied, "I don't know, but that's a damned good question." Sean looked at Mark questioningly. He hesitated. "You think you know already, right?"

"Maybe."

"And?"

"If the screen were metal . . ."

"Like gold or lead with a high K factor?"

"Like aluminum, or . . ." Mark paused expectantly.

"Compton shift." Sean beamed. "Son-of-a-bitch. Might work. Might produce electricity." He stopped. "But it would be inefficient as hell. Too much energy to produce the X-ray for the amount of electricity that you'd get out."

"And if the X-rays were free?"

"Might work. But where do you get free X-ray?"

"Just an idea. I'll talk more later. I gotta get over to Fred's. See you later." He disappeared down the staircase.

"Just an idea." Sean looked admiringly down the stairs.

CHAPTER SEVENTEEN
FARMING

Mark called Fred. "Hey guy, how'd you like to fly down to Marathon and tip a few with me and Paul?"

"You silly son of a bitch, you never get enough, do you?" Fred sounded odd. Was it relief?

"Never. So how about it, you got anything heavy going on?"

"Nothing that won't wait. See you at Oceanside in an hour."

When they met at the Aero Squadron, Mark explained his dilemma to Fred. "The long and short of it is this. I've had various offers, some in the form of money when I had cash flow difficulties. Later I had cash offers for stock, from people I never heard of."

"I understand." Fred nodded.

"I declined the loans because of high interest rates. I declined the cash because I was suspicious of where the money came from. Besides, Abraham has had the resources we needed."

"Right," Fred agreed.

"Now some people want to buy the whole thing." Mark frowned. "They're not my kind of people."

"Russians?"

"Be serious." Mark rubbed a finger around the rim of his

water glass. "They're hoods, crooks."

"So what's your point?" Fred showed no emotion. "Is their money green and is it a fair offer?"

Mark stared incredulously.

Fred grew quiet, focusing all his interest and attention on the king crab in front of him. He used the mallet on a leg, withdrew the meat, dipped it in butter, sucked it into his mouth and savored it. At last he put down the mallet, took a long pull on the Corona and looked at his young friend.

Mark broke the silence. "Fred, I don't understand how you can say that. You've always told me about the importance of being legitimate and honest in business."

"Remember J. Paul Getty, the richest man in the world. He wrote a book. He called it *How To Be Rich.* He told about a big deal that was important to him. Near the end he found out he was dealing with bad guys. He got off the airplane, turned around and never looked back, let the deal die and took his loss."

"Yes. He could afford to."

"That's not the point." Fred aimed his index finger right at Mark's head. "He said life is too short and our energy too limited to squander. With so many good deals ahead of you and so many good people to deal with, it's dumb to waste your extremely limited and precious time on bad deals or bad people."

"Great, so I give up what I've worked for." Mark shoved his plate.

"Not at all. But consider the alternatives. Say you went to the police. You hope you survive any physical attacks on you or the family or your employees. What if they blow up the plant? There's no way I can see that you're going to keep the company once they decide they want it. They'll either get it directly or destroy the company and sweep the remains into the sea."

"I just might not go so easy." Mark picked up a crab mallet as he gazed over at the Spitfire's wing suspended from the ceiling. He thought of Churchill's few men who'd held the might of Germany at bay.

"Look, Mark, don't get me wrong. I don't care if they blow you away." Mark's eyes snapped around just in time to catch the smile erupting on his friend's face. "But you bloody well are going to pay off that note before you go." He'd tried to sound lighthearted and had failed.

"Dammit Fred, if these guys are as lousy as you and everyone say, why aren't they in jail or dead?"

Fred shook his mallet at Mark. "Think about it, my friend. Every time they've been indicted, the witnesses die, disappear or refuse to testify. They've made total idiots of the Commission on Pornography and the sheriff. Who's going to knock them off besides other hoods? Hell, the drug dealers love 'em because of the broads. The guy on the street don't know and don't care."

Mark stared down at the scarcely touched crab legs on his plate. "Shit. Maybe Sean's right. Maybe I should take the money and run. At least you and Abraham and everyone would get your money."

"Son, I'm not trying to blow sunshine, but this may not be as bad as it seems. What the hell, they may make you a good offer and you might even like kicking back for awhile." Fred knew the offer would be good. It was their way.

"Maybe you're right." Mark retrieved his mallet and smashed a crab leg. "But it really pisses me off."

Now Fred broke the silence. "So how come we're going to Marathon?"

"I guess you're entitled to know, since I owe my ass to the company store. Paul has an idea for another business. He wants to run it by me on the q.t."

"If I were religious, I'd say the Lord works in mysterious ways."

"Did you say if?" Mark examined Fred's expression. Something eluded him.

"Come on Mark. You know what I mean. Maybe all this is a blessing in disguise."

"Yeah. And the Great Pumpkin is gonna visit me this year . . ."

"Okay, okay, but at least think about what I told you."

"I'll make you a deal. I'll let you fly your airplane, and you let me screw this up for myself." He thumped the pilot on the shoulder.

Silently Fred directed the Vari-Eze onto the strip. He prayed Mark wouldn't do something rash. Losing Billy had been enough . . .

When the prop quit spinning, they eased the plane into a small hangar at the end of the landing strip.

"You gotta be kidding," Fred huffed good-naturedly as he eyed the old yellow Volkswagen. The battery was dead.

"Do I look like I'm kidding? Help me push start this puppy and we'll cruise on over to meet Paul."

"Is this his idea of a joke?"

"No. It's cheap, easy, and if it gets ripped off, no one cares."

Fred shook his head, then steered as Mark pushed. Laughter erupted as he pictured his friends' reactions if they saw him now.

Fred remained bemused as he and Mark parked the beater VW and entered the restaurant.

"Check this." Mark pointed down the oyster bar where Paul was washing down a rock lobster with a beer and twist of lime.

"Hey, Captain." Mark waved, getting the massive Floridian's attention.

Paul cleared his throat ingloriously and beckoned Fred and Mark to join him. Mark wondered how many lobsters and how much beer it took to produce that greeting.

"So is everything set up for Walt?" Mark asked as he tried to get the waitress's attention.

"Yep. No sweat." Paul swung around on the stool. "Hey, Bonnie, more brew."

"Abe finally told me it was Walt who sent him." He shook his head and rolled his eyes. "What a couple of characters. Don't you just love em?"

"Top drawer dudes all right." Mark grinned. "But what's this deal you wanted to talk about?"

Fred ignored the conversation, focusing instead on the girls drifting in and out of the marina bar. "Damn. Damn . . . Damnnnn . . ." He motioned to Mark. "Hey, wanna come down for a shoot some time?"

Mark waved him off and returned his attention to Paul, who was showing off a small rock lobster.

"So what the heck is that, a little lobster?"

"Machrobrachaii Rosembergii," laughed Paul, "Giant shrimp."

"Get outta here. That has to weigh a quarter pound." Mark hefted the huge shrimp.

"More like a half a pound," Paul countered. "Succulent as an Australian prawn and we can raise them commercially."

Again Mark hefted the shrimp. "I like the idea, Paul. You say you can raise these monsters commercially?"

"You got it," Paul replied.

"Damn. If you and Sean want, I'll run the numbers on the computer. If it checks out maybe we could do something in Costa Rica or some other tropical area."

"Anywhere bananas grow and land is cheap," cautioned Paul.

"They can even be multi-cropped with rice and Talapia."

"Wouldn't that require pumps and electricity and fuel and a lot of infrastructure?"

"No. We could use local vegetation, or better yet, plant crops for food and bio-mass. We could power generators with steam from the bio-mass and even use the hot water for cooking, cleaning and . . ."

"You could have inexpensive sources for veggies, protein. You know Paul, profit aside, this could really be great for some third world countries. They could feed their people and still have a surplus to sell for hard currency. I like. I like it a lot. But it does sound a little like a biological perpetual motion machine."

"I'll get the basic info up to you right away and you judge for yourself."

"Sounds good." Mark uncoiled from the stool, extending his hand and ruggedly gripping Paul's. "I'll let you know soon all right." Mark flashed a thumbs up and headed toward the VW.

"Yoh, Fred. Let's buggie."

Back at Oceanside, Mark had an unexpected visitor, Jim Lopez. Fred quickly excused himself, leaving Mark with the policeman.

"No Jim, it's not what I had in mind. I'd like to see you earn a nice promotion, but not by solving my murder, thank you very much."

The Lieutenant removed his sunglasses. He looked carefully around as he polished the lenses. "Unofficially, Mark what I'd tell you is to cash out, if they make any offer you feel you can accept. Walk away from this. Find something else. Screw it. We both know half the hundred dollar bills in South Florida have coke powder on them and most of the rest have been through crooked banks or the porn industry."

As he replaced the glasses, briefly he looked over the lenses at his friend. "I'm telling you this. If the subject ever comes up, this conversation never took place and I don't know anything about anything. And that's the way it has to be. "

"I heard that. I know the official party line. If I do decide to take a run at these guys, you'll be the first to know."

"Do us all a favor. Take the money. Adios."

CHAPTER EIGHTEEN
SKIN DANCERS

Skin Dancers was situated in a freestanding shopping center on State Road 7. A gaudy yellow sign proclaimed adult entertainment and nude dancers inside. Mark screeched to a halt in the parking lot. As he jumped out of the Explorer and stretched himself to his full height, he determined that if the desert and the ocean had not defeated him, neither would these swine.

"You call it fun, I call it a laundry." Sean was probably right. As a cash business, the peep shows and nude bars associated with them provided an excellent place to launder mob money.

Nice, too bloody nice, he thought, as he examined the furnishings. The decorator had carte blanche. The paintings were probably real. Why not? Money was no object. Besides, in court it would be easier to claim an interest in art. First Amendment rights, and the whole bit. Legitimize the dump.

A burly maitre d' escorted Mark into the murky interior to the table where several men were arguing heatedly. At first he could not distinguish features. Gradually his eyes adjusted to the low light.

"Screw you, the Dolphins are finished. You bet with your own money."

"Mr. Trope, a Mr. Hansen to see you . . ."

Mark was disappointed with the man's appearance. His

clothing was expensive but didn't fit well. The $16,000 gold watch and jewel-bedecked pinky rings only cluttered any attempt to image understated elegance.

"Mark, please join me."

Trope motioned to the men flanking his table. Instantly they made way. Mark was seated facing his host. He extended his hand and flashed his best model's grin.

"Mr. Trope, a pleasure to meet you." The kid next door . . . Joe College . . . Apple Pie, Mom and the Flag. It would be fatal to show his true feelings. "Sorry to be late, but I just got in from a little marlin fishing and I haven't even been able to hit the office yet."

Trope's wimpy grip had no authority. His hand was clammy. How the hell had this scumbag gained such power?

"Look, I know your time is valuable, Mr. Trope, and I appreciate your seeing me on this informal basis. How may I help you?"

Trope steeled his nerves. "Well Mark, as you may know, for some time we've been interested in young and promising companies in South Florida."

Mark nodded.

"You may be aware that I'm the Treasurer of an entertainment company. This is just one of our places, and we want to diversify, particularly into growth opportunities. Preferably import-export."

Again Mark nodded.

"My associates favor high-tech, touchy-feely products. We feel that your company represents just the type of speculative investment that fits into our corporate objectives."

"And how do I fit into that picture?"

"Frankly, what we do is buy a company, pump in needed growth capital and then turn around and take the company public. If successful, we make a great deal of money." He paused, puffing on his cigar. "I tell you this so you'll understand our game plan as it were."

"I appreciate that. But . . ." Mark bored through the false facade. This guy was obviously nothing but a low life hood, who was paid to play the role of a Wall Street investment banker.

" . . . I of course have no plans for selling my company at this time. I'm young and I might enjoy seeing how far I can take the project." Mark struggled to sound like an airhead, but not an idiot. Trope must not realize he was being put on.

Trope wondered how a kid this young and gullible could have founded a company with the potential of the Locator. He paused, looking into Mark's eyes and thinking, Shit. If this guy is really as simple as he seems, we won't need to grab his girlfriend. Too bad. She'd bring big bucks in the Mid-East. His throat felt raw. He gulped his cocktail to brace his nerves. He was going to kick Adams's ass up around his ears when he got him alone. He must have bungled the first offer miserably. *Look what he's gotten me into. Damn his eyes.*

"Look Mark, you seem like a nice young man, let's not jerk each other around. I'm prepared to make a fair offer for your holdings, and all I ask in return is that you help me persuade your other shareholders to sell to me."

"Gee, I don't control what they do. And besides . . ."

"You see, Mark, we prefer to have complete ownership so we're free to develop a company along the lines we feel appropriate. We see you as a bright young man and we're not looking to hose you or screw you."

"Thanks, but —"

"I'll tell you what, subject to approval by my associates and your shareholders, how about we do this?" He puffed his cigar. "For your share of the company, we'll give you $1,580,000 and we'll agree to buy your shareholders' stock for twice what they've invested in cold cash."

"Well, I don't know . . ."

"Plus, we'll give you two dollars a unit for everything sold for the next 10 years. That's a buck for you and a buck to divvy up between the shareholders." Crushing his cigar on his plate, he summed up, "Stands to give them a damn fine return on their investment; you're all out clean, everybody's happy. Whaddaya' say?"

Mark was surprised at the generosity of the offer. Considering that Trope had the upper hand, they didn't have to try to be fair.

"Gee, Mr. Trope, that sounds pretty fair, but I don't want to sell my company just yet."

Trope scowled. Maybe Adams was right. This son-of-bitch was either dumb as a board or he had cast iron balls. He lit another cigar. "You know, my folks have to make something on the deal. You don't want to push them too hard, trying to make too much on your company."

Mark shook his head. "I don't think you're quite getting the picture here. I don't want to sell the company just now."

Trope rose. "Let me get my people on the phone. You can think it over one last time. Maybe we can persuade you to reconsider." Trope stubbed out the cigar in his cocktail glass.

Trope wasn't happy to give his next order. Desperately, he had wanted to undo Adams's blundered negotiations. He picked up the private phone in his office. "Okay, Terry. Grab her."

Mark watched Trope swagger back to the table. He'd have left, but the bodyguards made it clear that was not an option.

"So Mark, have you thought over what I said?"

"I have, and the answer is still —"

"Mark, one last time, $1,580,000 for you, plus royalties and we take care of your investors and employees."

"Sorry." Mark shook his head.

"I'll keep the offer open till noon tomorrow. Who knows? Maybe something will happen to make you change your mind. After that . . ." Trope let the sentence die as he puffed the new cigar.

When Mark got back to the plant he tried to call Linda. No answer. Probably down by the pool studying. He spent the afternoon with Ordean discussing Paul's shrimp project.

By four o'clock when he still got no answer at Linda's, he decided to drive down to Coconut Grove and surprise her. Only then did Trope's remarks flash back into his mind. He pressed hard on the accelerator.

Mark ran up the stairs. He froze at the doorway. The telephone was ringing and the door was ajar.

"Hello."

"Hello, Mark?"

"Yes."

"This is Jeannette Anderson. May I speak to Linda, please?"

Of all times for Linda's mother to call. Mark stared at the phone, cold sweat pouring from his body. "She's not here right now, Mrs. Anderson." He stalled. "I'm not sure exactly when she'll be home. Shall I have her call you?"

"Yes, please. And Mark — I'm sorry for what my husband said to you. You know, she's his little girl. I guess he's just not ready for a man in her life."

"No problem. I'll probably feel the same way when it's my daughter wanting to get married." He flushed as he realized how domesticated he sounded. "I'll have Linda call you."

Mark hung up, then dialed Lieutenant Lopez. "Jim, this is Mark." His voice wavered. "I think someone has kidnapped Linda. Yes, I'm in the apartment now." He scanned the room, then checked the bath and bedroom. "No sign of her anywhere. No signs of . . . of . . . a struggle."

"Why do I think she was kidnapped?" He kicked a chair across the room. "Well, the door was jimmied, she isn't here and a scumbag threatened me today. Other than that I can't imagine where I'd get such a paranoid notion."

Get a grip. Listen you . . . Mark tried to calm himself down. "Look, I'm sorry Jim. You tried to warn me. Now what the hell do I do?"

His head was pounding. He collapsed to his knees, suddenly exhausted. A heavy weight came down on his shoulders. "Jim, one more thing. I know this isn't your jurisdiction, but do whatever official bullshit needs doing. I'm just not up to it." Mark threw down the phone.

"Please God, let this be a misunderstanding." He leaned against the couch, his head whirling. "I'll gladly be the fool who overreacted when someone forgot to latch the door." Inside he knew the truth. His stomach churned. He wanted to retch. Holding his sides he headed for the bathroom, but couldn't make it.

Oh Christ. Maybe I shouldn't have called Jim, or any cops for that matter. He pictured the girl found in the trunk at the airport. He puked.

Was it too late? If he were truthful to himself, the most fun had already been had. The idea, the investors, the company . . . the product. From now on it would be routine business anyway, he weakly argued to himself. Not his favorite part of the game. Besides, even a kid learns better than to stand on the bow of a boat and pee into the wind. With the money he could do the big project, he and Linda . . .Linda. As he pulled shut the apartment door, bile boiled in his gut.

"Certainly, Mr. Hansen. Please have a seat. Mr. Trope will be with you shortly."

In hell, he will, by God, thought Mark.

"Well. Prompt I see, Mark." Trope extended his hand.

"Until noon you said."

"Yes. Let's go into my office where it's private." He led the way to the rear of the bar, then up to his penthouse office. "Mark, I hope we can count on your co-operation with the other shareholders. My people will honor the agreement and we will expect you to."

Mark couldn't comprehend how the word "honor" could pass this man's lips. The nausea from the previous day returned. Mark vowed he'd die before he'd let this swine see him puke.

"You know I am a man of my word," he hissed.

Trope studied the young man's features closely. "So I've been told." He paused. "And so are we. I believe we both have some phone calls to make. You might want to go to a friend's place to call your shareholders while I call, well, while I call some friends." He smiled at Mark and added, "All's well that ends well, my friend. No hard feelings."

Mark called the investors and quickly got their agreement to sell their stock. He would keep his word all right. But after

Linda was safe, he'd teach the scum-sucking bastards some new facts of life.

As for the investors, they were indebted to Mark, since without him their money would have been lost. Now they stood to make a big gain. No need for them to know who the buyers were. As long as the money was green.

CHAPTER NINETEEN
WHERE DEVILS TREAD

It should have been easy. Maybe Linda had fought a little too hard. Maybe she was just a little too pretty, too tempting. Maybe the kidnappers were too short a time out of the trees. No matter, Trope had a major problem. Linda was dead.

"Dead!" shouted Trope. "You stupid asshole. How could she be dead? All you had to do was hold her a little while." He gasped for breath. His hand shook as he pulled out another cigar and fired it. "Have you got any idea of the shit you've gotten us into? What am I going to tell Chicago? Do you think the boys in LA will be pleased? God-dammit, how am I going to explain this?" He sucked on the cigar repeatedly. "We may both be dead before she's had a chance to rot, you stupid son-of-a-bitch."

"Dammit Herm, it's not my fault. I've used these guys before. I don't know what went wrong. Don't blame me," whimpered Adams.

"All right, all right. Let me think. Okay, here's what you do." He paused, hand shaking as he raised his cigar. "Okay, you gotta clean up the mess. Leave nothing, I mean, absolutely nothing behind." His hand shook as he hung up. He broke out in a cold sweat. More calls to make.

"De Lisa, Trope. Yes, fine. The kid says yes and we're working out the details now. I'll get back to you. Yes. And tell

Mario Happy Birthday from Uncle Hermie. Yes . . . Goodbye." He sucked on the cigar. *God help me, if this don't get straightened out.*

"Mother of God, let this deal close before the kid figures out what happened." Trope remembered the saying about foxholes and atheists. It was true.

He hoped that even if the kid did catch on, he'd be sufficiently greedy to rejoice in the sale of the company and realize he could buy a dozen broads with his proceeds anyway. He'd fix him up with a couple of real stars. Broads that would make his dick hard and his memory short.

Giving up on the cigars, Hermine brought out a plastic bag. He snorted a little powder from his gold knife blade. "Hell, what's one chick more or less?" He felt better. "If they didn't have a pussy, there would be a bounty on the bitches anyway." He drifted, feeling much better. "Screw 'em all."

He dipped the knife again. "If worse comes to worse and he becomes troublesome, I'll have Adams snuff him." That would be messy and attract attention. "Don't want to piss off De Lisa. The brothers in Colombia, no biggie, they waste people all the time, sometimes just for shits and giggles. And the Russians, that was another matter. They were just plain crazy.

Adams's stomach was killing him despite the dose of Magatran. Damned ulcer. He'd already chewed a half dozen antacids. Cold sweat . . . he was soaking and shivering. "Let's go, William. We've got some carpet to clean." The hireling understood. There was a mess to clean up. He knew his job. He knew Adams.

Adams drove. "Damn Jamaicans. Screw up a simple job. Their fault . . . they pay." He parked the carpet cleaning truck by the house and waited for his assistants to arrive.

William scanned the house.

"Man, why they're so upset? Just a bitch. They can buy another." Marley sucked on the pipe. "They gonna pick her up?"

"Shit. Don't gotta buy, just share a little pipe . . . Get all you need." Elijah's head rolled. "Damn stray cat dies, you throw it out and get another, same with pussy." He giggled.

"Pick who up?"

"The bitch. What you think?"

"Screw you, gimma pipe."

William continued to scan the house. He looked at Adams in the rear view mirror.

"Never did like those two." He unpacked the submachine gun. "Got no class, no style. You know. Can't be trusted." He looked out the window. "What about the neighbors?" He screwed on a silencer.

"No sweat. Haitian one side, a Cuban the other. Speak no English, got no use for each other. Jamaicans behind 'em got nothing to do with any of 'em."

"Nice choice, sir. Should've worked." A craftsman's praise.

"Iron bars on all the windows?"Adams nodded. "Typical

Miami home." Sardonically he grinned.

"They're not going anywhere till we decide, then." He cocked the weapon. "How do you want it to go down?"

"They have guns. If they tumble to what's going down, it won't be fun. Not too bright, a little too fast on the trigger. Let's send in Hector and H'esus. They're expecting someone to clean up the mess. While they are distracted we'll get in and take them out."

"All of them?" He chose his words as carefully as bullets.

"Yes."

"Too bad. I thought those Haitian boys were coming along nice." He really liked the two illegals, especially H'esus.

"Good men are hard to find, it pisses me off to waste them. But this has to be thorough."

"There they go. Get ready." Adams chewed two more antacids.

Hector was first in. The house stunk. He knew the smell. Crack houses had a smell. "Where's the mess?" He grunted at the pipe smoker.

"There." Elijah pointed toward the bath.

"Sweet Jesus." He was riveted at the door. "Animals. Even Tonton Macout wouldn't do that." If he'd been better educated he might have pondered on the manpower shortages and on the slipping quality in the labor pool.

H'esus followed him into the bath. He took one look and vomited into the sink. "I don't like this. Not gonna do this again." He grunted. "God gonna punish this."

"Hey, give us a hand in here." Hector yelled to the Jamaicans.

As the four men struggled with the body and the carpet, Adams and the hireling slipped into the house unnoticed. Silently they moved into the kitchen. Hector was crying as he wrapped her body. Judging by the bruises and scratches on the two Jamaicans, she must have put up a pretty good fight. He just wanted to dump the body and vanish.

When the Jamaicans returned from the van, they re-lit a rock of crack. "Haitians and honkies, bunch of pussies." As they focused on their pipe, Adams and the other man stepped from the kitchen.

Like ducks on a pond, Adams thought.

The Jamaicans plunged forward, 45-caliber bullets exploding their brains. The hireling started setting time delay fuses on some plastic explosives. Adams doused the bodies with acetone. Carefully he opened a drum of ether.

"Nice touch, boss." The hireling strode to the van with Adams. "No prints, no body. Scumbags die in crack house shootout and fire. Film at 11." He nodded approvingly.

Adams popped another Magatran. "Head out Alligator Alley. We'll catch up with Hector after they dispose of the mess. After we finish with them, we can catch the show at Skin Dancers."

"If you don't mind sir, I'll skip that. Business and pleasure, you understand."

Adams turned, smiling. "I see your point. Anyway, I'll see you catch something extra for this one. The big guy appreciates good work."

The late movie had just started when Adams reported that he had cleaned up their little problem. He didn't detail his actions on the telephone, but Linda's body was placed in a stolen car and the car was sunk in a deep canal in the Everglades between Plantation and Naples. It would probably be months or years before the car and its contents would be discovered.

"You did good fixing up your mess, Terrance." Hermine stoked up another cigar. With any luck at all, the disappearance would be chalked up as a missing person. Even if Mark had his suspicions he couldn't prove that Trope had anything to do with it. It would be just another Miami incident. "But never muck up like that again, you know?"

Adams knew and he almost pissed himself when he looked back into Trope's eyes.

Trope was again feeling confident when he reported to his superiors. "No sweat. Hansen is recommending acceptance to his guy out of country. It's in the bag." He grimaced. "I know we paid heavy, but believe me, we'll make it back legit." Another grimace, "Relax, I'm telling you. I got it covered."

"Mark . . ." Daphne's voice shattered his concentration.

"What?"

"It'll be okay, I know it will. I just can feel it."

Aimlessly he put down the phone. Better stay at the apartment in case anyone tries to reach me, he thought. Linda will call from some isolated place where they'll leave her and then I'll go get her. Linda's parents, especially her father, weren't making things easy.

"Mark, I don't want to upset you," John Anderson snapped on the phone, "but we've called the police and filed a missing persons report. Where the hell is Linda?"

Mark inhaled, his shoulders lifting as he gathered momentum. "Sir, if I knew where your daughter was, do you honestly think I'd be on the phone with you now?"

Silence. Mark continued, "Mr. Anderson, it's not going to help matters if you and I are at odds. I love your daughter very much. I'm going to do everything I can to get Linda back safe and sound."

Jeannette broke in on the other line, "Mark," she reassured him, "we understand. He — we're just upset."

"Yes, of course."

"Mark —" Jeannette's voice broke. "No one is blaming you. Really."

"Thanks."

"I'm coming down there tomorrow," John barked. "It's the earliest flight I could get. We'll talk when I get there. But don't bother picking me up." The phone went dead.

Mark sat beside the phone cradling his head in his hands. What in God's name was he going to do? His own mother would call him a snake for doing business with Linda missing. If he didn't go through with it, she died. If he did, at least snake or not, Linda would still be alive. LINDA.

His jaw hurt. He realized that he had been grinding his teeth together. He stood up with difficulty, shaking his legs to bring back the circulation. Gingerly he worked his jaw.

Screw it. He'd better do something or he'd go nuts. He set the phone on call forward to his car phone and drove toward the plant. Daphne found him asleep on the couch the next morning.

"Damn. You scared me. I thought you were . . ." Her hand flew to her mouth, silencing the unuttered word.

"If it's any comfort to you, I feel worse than I look."

He wobbled to the bathroom and splashed water in his face.

"We gotta talk."

"Yes, we do. What is this all about, Mark?" She sat on the couch. "Have you heard from Linda?"

"No, dammit, nothing." Shaking his head he dropped into a chair and closed his eyes.

"Well, do you think . . .?"

"There's some things going on you need to know. The long and the short of it is this." He paused, searching for the right words. "The bad guys want the company. They have the money and they're willing to pay. I told them no way. They grabbed Linda. Myself, and the other investors have agreed to sell."

"What?" Incredulously she sank back in the couch.

"I've taken a big chance telling you. I also told Jim Lopez. I only told Linda's folks she's missing and we're doing everything we can to find her."

"Oh my God."

"Without going into detail, Fred, Sean and some other people all advised me it was the smart thing to do. I may have lost the only thing I ever wanted by trying to keep it all."

"Do you know when they'll let her go?"

"No. They're too smart to even admit they did it. It's all hints and indirection. They know I understand, but I can't prove a thing. We have to trust that they'll keep their part of the deal." He pounded the table. "Trust a sleaze bucket that would peddle kids for money?"

"Mark, surely Linda will be okay." She paused, "What will happen?"

"The company? They'll run it legit. That's their way now. Us? You and I get golden parachutes. My shareholders and I get healthy. That's about it." His voice was hollow.

"So what are we going to do?" She got off the couch and started to pace.

"I'm going to pray for Linda. And I'm going to handle the orderly transfer of the company to the new owners. I'd appreciate it if you did the same."

"You mean you're going to do what they asked . . . with Linda missing . . ." She hesitated. "I mean, I'm sorry . . ."

"That's all right. Nothing to forgive. You're right, really." A deep sadness puddled in his eyes. "It's just that I need to do something, keep busy. Surely they'll let her go. And if I stop . . ."

"I know. Me too. Nervous energy. I was cleaning the oven in my apartment at three this morning." She mustered a grim smile.

"I didn't picture you as so domestic."

"You don't understand. I mean I had it disassembled on the floor cleaning it." She smiled apologetically. "It helps me if I can work with tools when I'm upset. I just can't help it."

Even in his anxiety, Mark couldn't hold back a smile as he pictured Daphne tearing apart the whole kitchen in a fit of turmoil. "I drove around town half the night, praying for a phone call that wouldn't come," he murmured.

Trope played with the stone paperweight on his desk and stared absently at the gold nameplate "Hermine Trope." There was work to be done. Trope knew how to do it. Right. Right, he told himself anxiously. He had to disconnect from the abduction. Mark — or the police — must never suspect. He also knew he would have to maintain outward civility and internal toughness to see that the acquisition went smoothly.

He had to do this not only to keep Mark pacified, but to keep his connections calm. Trope was aware he was just as dispensable to them as the Haitians had been to him.

Trope called his banker. "Tony. Arrange to transfer a million seven to the acquisition account by Friday." He hesitated. "Screw the Feds. Screw cash flow. Just do it." He slammed down the phone. "Pissant."

I'll give the kid and his chums the cash, wire transfer the funds to the out-of-towners to seal the deal, and we'll finish the whole enchilada within three days. I'll be a damn hero.

He started to withdraw his plastic bag, but stopped short. *No, I think not. I'm still the boss. Let's keep it that way.* He was the boss.

CHAPTER TWENTY
ALLIGATOR ALLEY

"Stay there." The black man ordered his wife. "Don't you be coming over here now." He pointed at one child. Cautiously he laid his cane pole aside as he peered into the canal. "You kids stay with your mama." They ran back to his car.

He waded a short distance and looked below the surface. Then shakily he lurched back toward his family. Bile filled his mouth. He'd never seen a body underwater before. "Better flag down a State Trooper," he muttered, half to himself, "there's something real bad there."

From his perch on a burned-out tree limb, a buzzard had watched the entire scene, and realizing there was no profit in remaining, had taken flight for better pickings down the alley. Reaching a similar conclusion, the black man returned his tackle to the car and waited for the police. No way he'd eat anything he took out of that water.

"Hello, Detective Lopez. This is Dr. Charry from the Coroner's office. We have that Jane Doe, from the car accident out on the Alley. Your I.D. is probably correct. Trooper Parsons asked that I call." The doctor paused, continuing hesitantly, "How did you know the I.D.? This looks strange to me." Briefly he cited the autopsy results.

Jim listened to the details, shaking his head, his eyes misting over. "Long story, she's a friend of a friend." He paused thoughtfully. He started to ask further details, reconsidered. Some things are better left unknown. "Thanks for calling us. We'll take it from here."

Sure. Take it where? Shit. Jim stalked the room, pounding his fist into his palm. How the hell was he going to tell Mark? And what the hell was he going to tell him? Sorry Mark, your friend was found underwater with no water in her lungs. Oh don't worry. The car has hardly a scratch but she looks like she's been through a 110-mile-an-hour head-on collision.

He looked at the phone and ran his sleeve across his eyes ". . . positively identified the remains . . . notified Linda's parents . . . damn sorry . . . anything we can do . . ."

Mark was grateful he'd received the call in his apartment. He couldn't have borne the pain publicly. His senses shut down. He collapsed. It was the first time in years he broke down completely. The last time was in Saudi Arabia when his unit was headquartered near an air force unit. He was walking near a flight line of Apaches enjoying the sunset when he saw a child, a little girl about 10 years old skipping toward one of the aircraft. Civilians, even kids, weren't allowed on the flight line.

"Halt. Halt or I shoot." He was horrified.

"Stop. Stop, honey." Mark ran toward her. She continued.

"Brang." A warning shot; she headed toward the chopper.

"Brang." She died about nine feet from the strut. The grenade in her right hand rolled toward the Apache.

"Whomph." The detonation immediately set fire to the chopper.

"Son-of-a-bitch." The guard was staring at his partially severed hand.

"Why, sir? Why?" Just five days earlier, the little girl was in a group of children being entertained by this man's version of Pinocchio. "Why?" he pleaded.

Less than six months later Mark was home. They saved

the guard's hand but they couldn't save his life. Mark learned he'd killed himself in San Francisco ten months and eleven days later.

"Why? Who knows?"

The same feelings of frustration, rage and helplessness returned, magnified in intensity. It was so unfair. He had been spared his life only to be subjected to something worse.

"Why? Why would they kill her? I gave them what they wanted, they have the company." He fell to his knees. "Why . . ." He puked. Again . . .

The phone rang. "Screw it."

The doorbell rang. "Screw it."

He lay on the floor staring at the ceiling fan. Nothing mattered. Not the money . . . Not the plant . . . Not the locator . . . just Linda . . . he wanted to be with her.

At the end of the third day, Mark emerged from the apartment wearing the blue pin-stripe suit, a pale blue button-down oxford shirt and maroon tie. Ordean and Fred had handled the closing on the sale of Locator for him. He just could not be there. He knew that either he or Trope would have left the meeting in a body bag. Business before pleasure, he reassured himself.

He guided the Explorer to the barbershop. "George, I'll have a shampoo and styling. While you're at it, a shave and manicure." Style. Linda always liked style. He remembered.

Mark then drove to the plant and with the best grace he could muster he accepted the condolences offered by Joyce. Only Daphne had an inkling of what was processing. Mark determined to keep the situation under control, and if this meant people misunderstood, that was their problem.

"Joyce, please get Mr. Trope on the phone." He smiled, but it was a cheerless, icy smile. "Yes, sir."

Mark stormed into his office and waited to be connected. "Hermine, this is Mark. I thought we had an understanding."

"We do. I've done everything we agreed to. Your account's been credited, your people been paid, you got your contract."

"You know damn well that's not what I'm talking about."

"I swear to God, I don't know what you're talking about."

"It seems my fiancée had a terrible accident." His forearm hurt. No wonder. His hand was turning white. Deliberately he loosened his grasp. "Some senseless crime. The police have no idea who nor why. What do you think about that?"

"That's terrible, Mark. I'm truly sorry to hear of your loss. If there's anything we can do . . ."

"There is something you can do." Mark paused to let him wonder. "I've completed the arrangements with my engineer and the other employees." He paused, allowing Hermine to squirm. "I want to get away from here for awhile, now that the sale is done. Under the circumstances I don't think you and I should be working together. Bad memories and such. You understand."

"I understand. There will be no problem from us. I'm sure your people can handle anything we need done. But there is another matter we have not discussed."

Mark thought to himself, Here it comes.

"You did a great job of developing a product and we are sure that the production will be world class," he paused dramatically.

"And —"

"That still leaves the problem of maximizing sales volume."

Mark said nothing. He was calculating the wisdom of dealing with Trope in the hope of learning more about him and his bosses.

Trope continued, "The catch is that we need US Coast Guard approval so we can capture mass markets. And the lower level people have been very negative from what I understand."

"True. No doubt no one wants to stick their neck out for a new product."

"Whatever their motives, we think we have a way around the problem. We need your help for two or three days in Washington DC. It is not illegal, but it's in a gray area. You would be well paid."

"I really don't know about further involvement. Just what would I have to do, and what does this have to do with the approval process?"

Trope noticed Mark did not question the fee to be paid, only his involvement. He went on, "This is absolutely confidential. I am trusting you to honor that trust."

Mark almost laughed aloud at Trope using the words honor and trust, but he remained silent. Then he said simply, "Okay."

"You know that the Coast Guard is not like the other military services, it is under the Department of Transportation."

Mark nodded.

"The Secretary of Transportation has a wife who is a US Senator running for re-election. She needs campaign financing. It is possible that if we help her with her financial problems, that hubby will help us with our approval problems."

"Sounds illegal," Mark ventured.

"Not exactly. This is the gray area. We are not offering the Secretary a bribe. We simply are helping a Senator because we believe in her issues. If by a coincidence her husband helps us because he believes our product will save lives, well that is all right with us and it is not illegal," Trope suggested with undisguised glee.

"Why me? What makes you think I can get through to her? Anyway, I no longer am an owner and I have no connection with Locator."

"Exactly," Trope paused, "since you are not directly connected with Locator you are the perfect person to talk to her. You know all about the product but are not directly involved. There is no direct link between us and the Senator and the Coast Guard."

"I see." Mark certainly did see and he did not like what he saw. Yet . . . He did some more calculating. This just might play into his plans. "So why do you think she will see me, and exactly what do I have to do?"

"Well it turns out the Senator has a thing for handsome young men with red hair, something from the past apparently. Anyway, with your looks and our program we believe a deal can be made. You go talk to the Senator, politely but very carefully make our offer. If she buys the program fine, if not, so be it. What you do or do not do with the Senator is your business."

Mark had seen Trope in action and he did not for an instant believe that if the Senator refused it would be accepted so blithely. That was not his problem. "So if I agree to do this, what is in it for me, win, lose, or draw?"

At last, sighed Trope to himself, he's got his hand out. Aloud to Mark he responded, "You get 100K for making the trip, win or not. This is our way of expressing our appreciation for the honorable way you have conducted yourself."

Mark wanted to puke, but he kept his composure. "Look, it has been a bad week. I'd like to sleep on it."

"Mark I completely understand. Take your time. Take a couple of days if you need to. Just call me and let me know."

Mark's brain screamed, "Yeah, right, you understand. In a pig's ass you understand." He bit his tongue. Aloud, he said, "I'll let you know. Goodbye."

As Mark hung up the phone, Trope looked again at his desktop. He looked at the plastic bag. Slowly he opened his desk drawer and flicked it in. "He's in," he grinned as Adams walked in and seated himself on the sofa.

Since hearing about the body found on Alligator Alley, neither man had slept well. "The sooner, the better." Adams smiled back. With Mark compromised there was little likelihood of something else going wrong. Contented, he stroked Hermine's big poodle.

Mark left his office and paused at Joyce's desk. "I'll be in Montgomery for a few days. Linda's parents are driving over from Ramer. Her dad made arrangements to have her flown to Montgomery for the funeral." He felt bad for Joyce, but he had made sure she was protected financially. It was as much as he could do.

Dutifully Joyce took down the information Mark gave her. She wondered where she would work next. Mark was different; the plant was different. Nothing would be the same.

" . . . the family has a plot in the big city."

Sadly she watched her former boss wander into his office and one last time dial the phone.

Mark had never liked Alabama. It was not the people. They were warm and honest. Maybe it was the time he'd spent in the Army there. Now he had one more reason not to like being there. He stood at Linda's grave.

"Mr. Anderson, I realize we never had time to get to know each other properly. There's nothing I can say to you . . . and frankly there's nothing you can say to me that will make this any easier."

Mark grasped the older man's shoulders and forced his gaze upon him. "You've got no reason to believe me, but I swear to you that I'll get the people that did this. I'll get them if it takes all my money and the rest of my life, so help me God." He looked around making sure that only God and John Anderson heard him.

Linda's father staggered back as Mark released his grip. "I'll tell you what I do believe, Mark. I believe you'll try. God only knows why I believe you." As he turned to leave, he hesitated, then inched toward Mark and murmured, "You understand that I have to be there. I mean be right there, if God willing, I'm still around." He nodded toward his wife. "But she must never know." Mark nodded agreement. He watched John comfort his wife. He'd have been one hell of a father-in-law.

As the casket was lowered, Mark wished he were at liberty to explain to his friends why it was so important to him that they would meet him in Bimini. What had originally been planned as a wedding party was to have a much different purpose. He wondered how his friends would react.

He also wondered if Trope was still enjoying his little victory. Mark wept unashamed. Abruptly, drawing himself to his full height, he turned and walked swiftly to his waiting car. His tears burned away from his cheeks by the angry flush of his skin. First Washington, then Bimini and the meeting. He sped away.

CHAPTER TWENTY ONE
POOL SHARKS

Mark was suddenly brought back to the reality of his situation by the gentle splashing in the tub. He could not help wondering what Connie the Senator looked like in what he imagined was a very elegant Jacuzzi. It had been a desperate journey that brought him to this juncture. Now what?

"Mark," the voice emanated from the rear of the room.

"Yes,"

"Mark, please come here."

He hesitated. What the hell had he gotten himself into? If he went into the bathroom there was no telling what he would be expected to do, and he didn't know if he was willing or able to do anything. If he did not respond, there was little doubt in his mind that his mission was officially dead. Reluctantly he got up and walked to the door of the bathroom. "Yes."

"Don't be so bashful, it's all right, come on in."

He swallowed hard and entered.

His worst fears were realized. There she was buck naked in this incredible ornate tub. She smiled at him, not just that warm smile from earlier in the week. This was strangely different. Almost maternal. She motioned for him to sit by the tub. Since the only furniture available was the toilet, he perched on the pulled down seat.

"Don't be so stuffy. I won't attack you and I don't bite." She moved a sponge down one arm and over her shoulder. "I think much better when I am relaxed in a nice hot tub. Some people pace, some smoke and others drink, I tub."

Mark relaxed a little, but he was absolutely baffled.

"Mark, despite the exterior, I am a battle-hardened veteran. There is not too much I have not seen or heard or for that matter done. I know my reputation and I know one hell of a lot more about you than you may imagine." She continued to move the sponge over her neck and shoulders. She looked her age and on her it looked marvelous. Despite the events of the last weeks it was impossible for Mark not to appreciate her beauty.

"Thank you," she continued. "Some men pour out the compliments in words, you do it with your eyes."

Mark actually blushed. My God, he felt like a schoolboy.

"I find you very attractive," her voice grew mellow, "and if we both choose, we can fuck each other's brains out later. Or not. But first we need to have a serious private conversation."

Mark no longer felt like a schoolboy. He was by now totally confused. Was Connie a bimbo, high up on the food chain but still a bimbo? Or was she on some sort of weird maternal love trip? He thought back to Trope's remarks.

"Get out of your clothes and join me in the tub so I can be sure you are not wired," Connie commanded.

Quickly he complied, but it was not in some sexual heat. Rather, it was some deep curiosity as to where this would lead and how it would play out.

Every time he thought he had seen it all, experienced it all, he was proven completely wrong.

"It is less dangerous for me to have a reputation as an eccentric wild woman than to be thought of as a crooked politician. My colleagues regularly debauch themselves and that is accepted. What is not accepted is taking bribes for political favors and getting caught at it." She continued to play at washing herself with the sponge.

"But, I have not offered . . ."

"Please, don't go there. We're grown-ups. I know what

your associates need and your associates know what I need. Given the events of the past few weeks, the only thing that puzzles me is why you are still involved and what your intentions are. You cannot imagine you got this close to me or my husband without being checked out very carefully."

"I told your husband that I would only speak for myself and you would have to draw your own conclusions about anyone else."

"That doesn't completely answer my question."

"Maybe I can't answer your question." He reached across and gently took the sponge away from her. He raised her left leg, exposing her foot above the water line and began to softly massage it with the sponge.

"Maybe you don't want to," she eyed him from partially closed lids.

"Maybe."

"Let's be candid, just for a little while, just here, just now. You have nothing in common with those people. I understand who and what they are. I may be willing to use them and let them use me. They have their type of power and I have mine. That is politics. But what the hell is it with you?"

Mark paused, squeezing the sponge hard in his hand. "Why do you want to know?" Mark studied her closely wondering just how much, if any at all, he could trust her.

"I could be very romantic and tell you that you remind me of someone I cared for very much and could not help, and that is the reason I want to help you. And maybe there would be some truth in that." She offered the other foot and eased down in the tub slightly.

"Or you could have some other reason."

"I could. If I did, you probably would never know unless I told you and you believed me. That would take a lot of trust on both sides."

"And . . .?" Mark squeezed water over her right foot, sponged and squeezed.

"And we don't know each other quite that well yet."

"So."

"I know what I'm getting involved with when I deal with them. I am just not sure what I'm getting involved with when I'm dealing with you." She gazed directly into his eyes as if challenging him.

"You are not getting involved in anything with me. This is strictly business. I think you know why, if you really know as much about me as you implied."

"I can accept that. You can inform your associates they have a deal. As for you and me, that is still an open question." She reached over and took back the sponge. It disappeared beneath the water. "I think you would be more fun to ride than a wild bull. I think it would be a dangerous ride for both of us." She moved the sponge up his thigh.

"Just how much do you really know?" he asked bluntly as he involuntarily moved toward her.

"I know that you loved your Linda just as much as I loved my Andy. I know neither one of us will ever have them back and it makes both of us mad enough to die." She backed off slightly and looked through his eyes straight into his heart. "So we both do what we have to do to get through the days and the nights. I have an understanding husband and more power than you can imagine. It helps." Now she moved close to him.

Mark grabbed her. At first he did not know whether to choke her for even daring to mention Linda's name, or to love her for sharing a passion so deep that others could not imagine or understand it.

"I know Mark, I know." she whispered.

He stood up, quickly pulling her up with him. He lifted her from the tub and spread her like a carpet on the bathroom floor. They fucked violently and long. It was not about love. It was about passion lost and relived. It was about escape from a reality that was simply too terrible to bear.

The next afternoon Mark boarded his plane for the Islands. One down, one to go," he thought.

At rest in the warm clear waters off Bimini, the Reef Ruler

looked as if it were a natural extension of the waves. Sleek and fluid in appearance, it echoed the friendly lapping of the water.

Jeanne-Marie looked up toward the ship's bridge. "Abraham has this made well, n' est-ce pas?"

Not too many 60-footers in your country my dear?" Sean chided the lovely Angolan.

Splashing him with warm water from the hot tub, Jeanne-Marie laughed. "You Americans. So impressed with anything big and expensive. We really must talk about your values, you capitalist lackey."

"Don't see you refusing to use the hot tub or drink the Lafite Rothschild," Paul chimed in from the hammock.

"Careful Paul. The last guy that ruffled her tailfeathers got thrown over the side," Sean warned his friend, only half in jest.

"His choice, as you say," Jeanne-Marie injected as she rose from the tub to enjoy the sunny afterdeck.

Sean reclined in the chaise and sipped his Absolute and tonic water. He'd admired the strength and agility of many women in many sports, but he'd never seen a woman with such upper body strength and fluid stealthy grace. The contradiction between the grace and power remained a mystery to him.

"So did Mark say what he wanted us here for?" Paul wanted to change the subject. He looked at the girl. He could kick her butt over the rail any time but he'd look like a jerk doing it.

"Yes. We're supposed to keep you out of trouble until Mark and Daphne tell us the big secret," Sean laughed.

"You haven't figured this out yet, my friends." Jeanne-Marie removed her bikini top and reclined on the deck to sun. No tan lines showed.

Paul wasn't sure if he was more disturbed by the remark or the removal. Silence is golden, he thought as he admired the girl from the safety of his silvered sunglasses.

"We'll all know everything soon. If their flight is on time we'll know very soon." Sean finished his drink and joined Paul in admiring the scenery of the Bimini inlet.

"Damn. Can you do something about that motor?" Paul moaned from the fishing chair.

"I can't hear a thing. You must be having tremors and it serves you right," Jeanne-Marie scolded. She rose, jiggled over to Paul and placed a wet cloth on his forehead. "Maybe you aren't so young as you once were."

"Must have been some bad wine," Paul muttered. "Anyway, I think Mark is nearly here." He cupped his hand to his ear. A small outboard motor could just barely be heard over the lapping of the waves. Jeanne-Marie wondered if a hangover made Paul's hearing more acute.

"Ahoy," came a voice from the bow. It was Mark.

"Back here," responded Jeanne-Marie.

Daphne and Mark picked their way through the equipment stowed on the deck. They paused on the rear deck.

"New kind of sunglasses?" Mark jibed at Paul, who had slid the wet cloth down over his eyes.

"Up yours," groused Paul. "When are you going to tell us why you dragged our butts half out here?"

"Soon as everyone gets here," Mark replied.

Something in Mark's voice prompted Paul to raise the cloth and scan his young friend deliberately. "Hope it was worth it," Paul added, hoping to pry more information from Mark.

"Just look at the spinner dolphin." Daphne changed the subject. "Isn't it beautiful?"

"Nice try." Sean's voice came from above.

Mark, Paul and Daphne looked toward the tower. They could just make out Sean's torso in the glare. Shielding her eyes, Daphne called, "Quit hiding up there and join the rest of the casualties down here."

"It's safer up here. One of you drunks may barf on me down there."

Now that's rude," Mark yelled. "Walt would be shocked to hear you talking that way."

"It'll take more than that to shock me," came a second voice from above. It was Walt, but he wasn't visible in the glare.

"Some hosts we are," Mark commented to Daphne. "Last ones here at our own party."

"Didn't know it was a party." Sean slid down the ladder.

Walt followed Sean down the ladder. "Nice place, but a strange time for a party, if I may say so."

"For this party, the perfect time," came the mysterious reply, as the Captain started the boat's engines. "Abraham has volunteered Andy to be our skipper today, so we can take care of business."

"So which is it, business or party?" bellowed Paul as he sat up in the fighting chair.

"Both," Mark answered firmly.

Sean looked at Daphne. She returned his gaze with a look and lift of the eyebrows that clearly said, "Beats the heck out of me."

Andy revved the twin turbo diesels and headed the Reef Ruler away from the inlet. He proceeded to the coordinates Mark had plotted, then throttled back the engines and dropped anchor. At last Mark turned and faced his friends assembled on the afterdeck.

"When I first planned this trip, it was intended as a stop-over on my honeymoon. This is where Locator was born. This is where . . . many things were born." Self-consciously he looked down, avoiding their eyes. "Well, obviously that was not to be. Sean, your family was Irish Catholic, and Jeanne-Marie, your mother was Catholic, so maybe what I propose won't sound too crazy to you." He nodded toward them.

"I wish to treat this gathering as a sort of wake, if you will. All of us who knew and loved Linda can celebrate her love of life, and her memory." He choked on the words.

"Before we do that, I wish to speak to you of business, of unfinished business." He hesitated, making sure he had the attention of his friends.

His green eyes had darkened and his face had taken on a strange cast, not malevolent but . . . but what? Daphne shivered. Sean was also unsettled by his friend's expression. "What's up?" he whispered to Daphne.

"Jesus," she murmured. "I really don't know."

"I've seen that look in combat." He shook his head. " . . . unfinished business."

Mark continued. "You know that I sold my business, our business, under duress. I was to get Linda and the money in exchange for the company." Slowly he moved closer, his eyes traveling around the circle of friends. They watched him, aware of the building tension, feeling the charge in Mark's voice, the meaning behind his words.

"What I tell you now, I will say only one time. I will deny it was said. You must do the same." Together they nodded agreement, not knowing what they were agreeing to.

"When I nearly drowned in these waters, I swore that if I were spared I would do something to help other people. The first step was the Locator. I kept my word." He hesitated, eyes tightening. "When Linda died, I swore she would be avenged. I will keep my word."

"Holy shit," exclaimed Paul.

"Whew," uttered Sean.

"Oh my God," added Daphne.

Jeanne-Marie smiled widely. She already understood why Mark had invited her.

"You're right, Paul." Mark looked squarely at his friend. "Holy shit, indeed." Again scanning the circle, Mark continued, "When I started Locator, I needed help. I got it in abundance. More than ever, I'll need help now." He gestured reassuringly. "I don't ask for, nor do I expect any direct assistance. But I do need indirect help."

"Sean, you and Paul and Walt will understand when I say I need intelligence information and logistic support. Jeanne-Marie, you've already figured everything out." He turned to Daphne.

"Daphne, you have the hardest task of all. I must ask you to continue the orderly transfer of Locator until it is successful." He directed a solemn smile toward her. "That was the bad news. The good news—it is my pleasure to announce that Abraham and myself are forming a new company. We're hoping that you,

Daphne, will join us as management engineer. We want you to run the company in Fort Lauderdale for us, as soon as you can finish up at Locator. I wanted to share with all of you my personal business plans for the next few years and to invite you to join with me if you like."

In turn he addressed his friends, "I hope that you, Jeanne-Marie, will help us with import-export activities." She nodded.

"Sean, we know that you and Paul already are well pleased with your present situations, but we would welcome your input in setting up operations and design matters."

"No worries, mate," said Paul.

"Walt, we'd welcome your participation in distribution and manufacturing in the Japan or Taiwan areas. We plan to start out with an aquatic toy —The Pool Shark. Then a toy submarine, and then we'll see what develops. After we've partied for a few days we can discuss this in more detail, but I just thought you should know everything that's on my mind."

Mark paused, assessing the response from each of them. If he read them correctly, these friends and partners were not only going to do their damndest to help him; they would try to make it work – everything — everything.

"I will be living in New Zealand for a while. Abraham and I have some other business to attend to. I'll talk with each of you individually about certain other matters. Having dispensed with business, may I now suggest we enjoy a hair of the dog that bit some of us last night."

For a time Mark leaned against the bow rail, then turned to Sean, Walt and Paul. "We have to make sure that no one be able to relate any subsequent acts to us. This is particularly true in my case, since I have the strongest and most obvious motive. Therefore, whatever is accomplished will have to be achieved while all of us are well away from the scene.

Paul interrupted, "Is all this mystery and razz-a-matazz necessary?"

"In every criminal investigation there are certain key elements that must be proven; motive, means and opportunity must be shown. If one or more elements are missing, then proof becomes impossible. So the answer is yes, it is necessary."

"Fine." Sean, appraised Mark sternly. "But what I'm warning you about is this. I've seen some men crumble, dying with their weapons unfired. Next to them, men having expended all their ammunition, fought to their death with bare hands and entrenching tools." Sean hesitated for this to sink in.

"You never know how someone will act under stress. That means you and anyone involved with you." He wasn't quite certain how to evaluate Mark's response. "We all know the risks. For myself, if anyone had harmed Barbara or our daughter, Mark would do no less for me."

Paul coolly smiled agreement; he loved a good fight and as long as Sean was in, he was in.

"What about the Angolan?" Sean probed.

"Jeanne-Marie has been through revolution and turmoil in her native land, sort of like Iraq. She's no stranger to death, violence or revenge." Mark paused. "Her parents died at the hands of drug lords from Russia during their struggle to take over the government. Her dad was a career diplomat."

"Let me see if I get this correct." Sean's eyes narrowed. This girl is your sword of Pericles."

"Close, but no cigar." Mark smiled. "She has motive and I can supply opportunity. But, I was serious when I said no direct involvement."

Sean relaxed.

"Not for the reasons you may think," Mark continued pointedly. "She has skill, guts and motive. She's fluent in five languages and . . . well, you've seen her. She can gain access to any male-dominated enterprises with ease."

Yeah. And what happens to her if someone catches on?"

"Jeanne-Marie has seen depravity and degradation. You know what it was like in the Mid-East. It was worse in Angola."

"That was then, this is now."

"Agreed. But she wants to help me now, so that I can help her later. She has her own agenda. Frankly, I don't know the details and I'm not sure I want to."

"Fine. But remember what I said. She knows a lot. If she's caught it wouldn't be good for either of you."

"I'll remember that."

Mark resumed. "Again, the greatest risk is at the point of attack. Militarily this is a key to achieving victory, the superior force concentrated at the correct place and the right time, will produce triumph." They comprehended. Mark saw. He also observed that evidently they shared his determination to stage and execute an expert performance. "Let's rejoin our friends. Enough of this for now."

Mark came up behind Daphne, who was staring absently at the computer screen. "Why so pensive, Penelope?"

"Oh!" She turned. "You startled me."

"Second thoughts?"

"You know better than that." Daphne frowned. "But, I hope you really have thought about this carefully. You know there's an old saying, 'When you go to kill an enemy in revenge, first dig two graves.' "

Grinning, Mark corrected her, "It's a Greek saying, and oh, never mind . . ." Reconsidering, "Look, I know you would've helped, just for Linda, but there'll be no hard feelings from anyone if . . ."

"I beg your pardon, but it is a British saying, and I'm here because I want to be." She resumed work at the terminal.

The next months passed in a blur of activity for Daphne. Abraham incorporated the toy company in Auckland. Daphne guided Locator until American Entertainment sold the company to a large multi-national firm. Just as Mark had been told, they built it and sold it, at a big profit. Of course the Coast Guard approval didn't hurt.

Daphne then worked from a small office near Sean's Hobbies. Since they decided to have toy production done in the Pacific Rim, she needed only design equipment and office space in the United States. For convenience Mark kept his old apartment, but was rarely there, since he was out of the country or away from Lauderdale most of the time.

Daphne spent far more time in the office than Mark, since she was busy designing tooling and equipment from the sketches prepared by Mark. Still he often occupied her thoughts.

"Don't you wonder where he goes or what he's doing?" she asked Sean one day when they were discussing Mark's hectic schedule.

"No, I don't." He reached across the computer terminal and gently touched her hand. "And neither do you."

It's ironic, thought Daphne, relaxing in the office after an exhausting day, Mark never would've set up the toy company, except for the need to cover his activities. She returned the toothy grin of the retail packaged Pool Shark on the table. Deliberately, she picked up the prototype toy submarine. Now, almost by accident, the company was developing so well it might be more profitable than Locator. "Only in America would a toy sell more dollar volume than a life saving device," she thought. Across from her, Mark relaxed and admired her handicraft. She enjoyed his visits so much, she wished they could be longer and more frequent.

Mark admired the subtle detail in the new prototype. Daphne did superb work. Gently he reached over and took the sub from her grasp. As he fingered the submarine he thought, *A little more than a year ago I was aimlessly wandering. Now . . . we succeed.* It's so easy . . . He thought of the talented engineer who had contributed so much to his success. He thought of the risks she had taken to help him, and . . . guiltily, he thought of Linda and his unfinished business.

CHAPTER TWENTY TWO NATURE'S CHILD

"Welcome aboard Mr. Trope . . . Mr. Adams." Hermine looked down 178 feet of polished deck.

"Thank you. Its good to be aboard, Captain."

"Your party is expecting you in the salon."

"Excellent. Prepare to get under way." He led his brother-in-law down a spiral staircase. "Damn Swedes know how to build a boat!" He fingered the banister rail.

"How fast is it?" Adams asked.

"Who gives a shit? If I want to go fast, I'll take the Cougar." Disparagingly he shook his head.

"Jeez Herm, I didn't mean nothing."

Seeing the hurt look, he mollified his associate, "Well it does have two 1250 hp turbo-charged diesels. Electric power is provided by two 45 kv and one 75kv generators." Adams brightened. "She has the latest in electronic navigation and entertainment equipment— completely computer controlled for ease of operation."

"Good thing," Adams offered. "Damn Panamanian crew can't pour piss out of a boot with directions on the heel."

"Did it ever occur to you that I chose foreign registry and a mostly foreign crew for good reasons?" He wondered if it was worth the trouble of explaining. "Like I want privacy, for example."

"Oh, yeah, I see." Whenever Hermine was on board there was an ample supply of females to keep him company and to fill the needs of his guests.

Trope stopped at an intercom. "Captain: You may take us out past the three-mile limit." He smirked at Adams. "Let's party." In the tourist season many of his influential Northern friends would visit. He wanted to be ready.

"May I take it that we're properly supplied?"

"Powder and pussy," Adams beamed. "We could shoot a film right here on board if you want. Nothing far out, but good commercial stuff."

Smiling, Trope triggered the intercom again. "Hey, Cap — How's the weather looking?"

"No sweat, sir. Seas two to three feet, no more than 20% probability of rain. Couldn't ask for better."

Nature's Child had been out for about sixteen hours when the captain uneasily checked his charts. "Jim, come on up pronto." His navigation equipment seemed to be acting up. The mate was expert on electronic navigation.

"What's the beef, Ralph?"

"Look. The satellite navigation says we're only three-and-one-half miles out. Now look outside. Does that look like three miles?"

"What the —" He couldn't pick out any familiar lights or landmarks.

"No problem. The automatic pilot's tied into the sat nav and the main computer. Let's check the print out." He scowled.

"Something is wrong, we're off course but the automatic alarm failed to trigger. It should've rung when our path deviated from predicted, by more than 100 meters."

"Dammit. The computer must've screwed up."

"Get the electronics technician up here on the double. I want this thing fixed ASAP."

"What's the problem, skipper?" The technician careened into the cabin.

"Aside from your sloppy appearance, mister, the navigation gear has gone haywire. Fix it."

"Yes sir." He hoped he could. He was feeling like shit. The crack was still screaming in his lungs. His whole body was messed up. "Damn that French bitch anyway. I should've never let her talk me into . . ."

"Today. If you don't mind, sailor."

"Yes sir." The urge to go back to sleep in his cabin was strong; the urge to stay alive was stronger. He set out to get a fix on their location and see if he could raise any other vessels in their vicinity on the radio.

"Damn." He swore. "All right. Very funny. Who's been screwing with the radio?" Instead of transmitting and receiving on its assigned bands, it was locked onto a Cuban propaganda channel.

"The output meter says we're not putting out any signal at all. And the friggin secondary radio is locked on the Voice of America. More propaganda."

In desperation he struggled to the port side where two emergency boats, 25 foot Boston Whalers, were suspended from davits. "Son of a bitch. Who's the wise guy?" The emergency radios stowed on the boats were not operating.

"Juan." He called a cabin boy. "Check the emergency radio in the crew quarters while I get back to the navigation room. Something is very wrong." He had to tell the captain.

"Sir, there's no way a systematic failure of that many pieces of equipment would be accidental." Even in his less than perfect state, he realized someone was playing a not very humorous prank; or they were in serious trouble.

"Captain, I think the electronics have been deliberately screwed up."

"General Quarters." The captain barked into the intercom.

"Security alert. This is not a drill." Alarms rang everywhere.

"Guards to the salon. See to the safety of the boss and his guests until the ship is secure."

He switched the radar to long range scan and saw no ship or aircraft traffic that seemed threatening. Then he shortened the scan and looked carefully for any indication of a threat closer to the Nature's Child. The radar was clear.

"All hands, secure the vessel against a possible attack. And for crying out loud, bring me an operating radio transmitter."

They had six short range vhf transceivers that were used for on board security communication. Surely one had to be working.

"Mr. Trope, are you all right down there?" Hell for all he knew, one of Hermine's competitors might have decided to —

"Yeah. What the hell's going on? You just interrupted the best strip poker game I ever filmed." Gently he chided the Captain. In his business he couldn't go to the courts, the Chamber of Commerce or the government if he felt a competitor was engaged in unfair trade practices.

"No sign of any cowboys, sir." Again he scanned the radar screen. "Nothing anywhere near us."

"Okay, just make sure all portholes are fastened down and all watertight doors are secured." He paused. "And have the mate do a weapons check. We're sitting ducks out here."

From the weapon's lockers, the security guards had pulled out high-powered rifles with telescopic sights and night vision devices.

"Good thinking, guys." Jim checked the rest of their equipment. They had riot shotguns and Uzi submachine guns for close-in work above decks, and GLOCK 19 shot semi-automatic 9mm pistols for work below decks.

"Which one of you guys has the smoke grenades?" A hand shot up. "Make damn sure you don't pop one of those unnecessarily. They stink up the place."

Jim checked their flack jackets. There was nothing subtle about their approach. It was strictly military.

"Keep the navigation lights on. The captain doesn't want to attract unneeded attention from the Coast Guard." He snapped a pseudo military salute. "Carry on."

They needed information and maybe they needed help, but they did not need the Coast Guard or U. S. customs officers examining their vessel.

"Terry," Trope ordered. "Go to the special locker and break out two LAWS rockets. Set them one port and one starboard in case someone gets in close with a high speed boat or with a helicopter."

"Go all the way. Lay out the smoke projectors in case we need to hide."

Trope remained calm. It would take a very determined and well-armed adversary to penetrate their defenses. Nothing short of a small military vessel would be smart to attack them. The Nature's Child might be compared to a porcupine. It bristled with short-range defenses, and although docile by nature, it could give a good account of itself if attacked.

"Cap, how's the radar looking?"

"Right now there are only two blips. Probably 18 to 25 foot fishing boats. They won't get anywhere near us."

"Look at that, Jim." He pointed to the dots. "There's always nuts going out to the Gulf Stream with single engine fishing boats." He sighed. "We'll see them listed missing in the paper. Lucky ones get recovered after many helpless days at sea. Dumb asses."

"The boat's secure, Hermine," Adams reported. "All men are at their duty stations and there's no sign of any threat. "

Adams was absolutely correct. They were in no imminent danger from any outside force.

At 12:17 in the evening the sudden secession of the main power plants slowed down Nature's Child and she lost steerage way. High above an albatross lazily blinked in response to the sudden silence and then glided on.

"Jim, get below to check out the engine room. Tell me what you find." The captain's shirt was soaking wet. Fatigue showed darkly under his eyes.

"Engine room. Get off your duffs and get the engines back on line," he screamed. "It's a long swim to Panama." He relented.

"The mate's coming down to help you."

By the time Jim reached the engine room he found three

men scrambling desperately over the power plants. One Cuban was mumbling out loud. He understood enough Spanish to recognize the mumbling as a prayer to the blessed virgin.

Reneaud, the senior man, said, "There's nothing wrong with the batteries and we're checking the fuel system right now."

Nearly two hours later, the mate reported, "Captain, the computer controls for the fuel and ignition systems failed. We tried a spare board, but when we replaced it, the damn thing went up in smoke." He said nothing about the Cuban's burned hands.

"We'll try the second back-up board. If that fails, the only thing left is to by-pass the computer controls and jury-rig something to get us back to port." He waited.

"Jim, you know we're in serious shit drifting like this. Do your best." He paused. "And Jim, thanks. You're doin fine."

At l: 24 in the morning the main induction pipe, a six-inch steel feeder for the desalinating unit that provided fresh water for the ship, malfunctioned. A large two-way valve opened. Sea water started to flood the compartment. For no apparent reason the alarm system ignored the emergency. A fierce stream of water was pouring in through the large diameter pipe below the waterline of the ship.

The water began to fill the compartment, then started on the adjoining one. Despite the fact that the watertight doors had been secured, openings in the bulkheads for new security system piping, not yet installed, gave access to three compartments in addition to the water purifying one. The flood-alarms in all three compartments continued to ignore the rising water level.

Shortly after 2:00 a.m., the main exhausts from the engines to the sea opened up and streams of water started to flood the engine compartment. The crew members bravely struggled with the emergency and were able to eventually rig a seal around the pipes to control the flooding. But their victory celebration was short-lived. The smell of diesel fuel started to fill the room and they quickly realized that somehow the fuel tanks or fuel lines had opened up. At least it wasn't gasoline or hydraulic fluid. The danger of an explosion below would have caused them to abandon their efforts and head above deck.

"... Mary, mother of God ..." The Cuban intensified his prayers as he resolutely looked for the fuel leak. Meanwhile his Panamanian companions joined him in prayer. Albeit to different gods or at least in different languages, their pleas bore the same message.

"Evie, what the hell's going on? Why is someone trying to wreck the ship?" the model asked her new friend.

"Lord I don't know. I'd never come if I'd known this," she grumbled. "Dammit, I spent a fortune on my hair and nails."

"What're you broads whispering about?" Adams demanded.

"Don't be so edgy, honeychild, we're just a little nervous, you know."

"Take it easy, Terrance," Hermine soothed. "Of course they're nervous." He turned to his companions. "Relax ladies. You're in good hands." He fondled Evie's breast.

"Oh Hermine," she giggled.

Anxiety heightened as they awaited the reassuring sound of running engines. Who could predict with any certainty what would happen next?

"Captain, just in case, have both emergency boats swung out on their davits. Lower them so they're ready." He hesitated. "And make sure they're checked."

When the starboard boat was swung out on its davit, bow first it dropped down, banged against the ship's side, rolled over and fell into the sea.

"What friggin next?" the captain fumed. "Find out what happened."

Again the culprit was an electronic control, the one that regulated the hydraulics for the davit system.

"Check the other boat."

A careful inspection of the port side boat revealed it too was in danger of being released prematurely. By a stroke of luck it held and was not dumped into the sea. It took nearly forty-five minutes but the crew was able to rig a block and tackle on the front and rear of the boat, enabling them to lower it to the seas and subsequently draw it to the stern where the dive ladder and platform were located. At that point it would be easier to get off the ship from the stern to get into the small boat. Adams transferred small arms as well as food, water and electronic gear to the Boston Whaler. He test started both engines to make sure in the event they were needed for escape that the outboard engines operated correctly.

Adams was not simply being the good servant. He wanted to make damn sure he had an escape route. It was not so much loyalty as enlightened self-interest that dictated his diligence in preparing the Whaler for use.

"Bong . . . Bong . . . Bong," The alarm sounded at 3 a.m.

"Firelight from the bilges, sir," Jim reported.

"So what else is new?" He sounded relieved. "At least we know . . . what the hell . . . the automatic fire extinguishing system failed to operate."

"I'll use the manual override, sir."

A dull thud followed by more alarms.

"I don't even want to know." The captain shook his head.

Trope stared at Adams. "Someone damned clever is doing this." His voice reflected grudging admiration.

"Let's not underestimate the bastard."

Probably the Libyan, Adams thought. Retribution for the blonde he sold him. How did he know she had AIDS? Kind of funny really. Not even his money could save him. Wonder how many others she infected?

Trope couldn't attribute this thoroughness to any of his American enemies. Not even the New Yorkers or Californians were so subtle or efficient.

"Terry, you ever hear of hamanata?"

Adams grinned goofily.

"Give it a rest. It's a Mid-East custom of killing everything belonging to an enemy. Nothing is left alive at the scene of the raid. Not man . . . woman . . . child . . . dog . . . cat . . . not even a flea."

Adams blinked.

"It's the ultimate message. The purpose is to demonstrate the futility of crossing the power responsible."

"I don't know where this shit is coming from, but we're not going to be pulled like a root, my friend. Have you made the arrangements for us to leave safely?"

"We have a boat, food, weapons, everything we need."

"Make damn sure our back door is covered."

"Give me a minute to check the passages and we can leave any time you want."

"I want," he commanded.

Adams gestured to the mate, "Jim, take the girls and wait for us in the Boston Whaler." He checked the passageway, then escorted Trope to the ladder. As they climbed down the ladder Hermine again asked, "Who do we know clever enough to do this?"

"Beats the shit outta me. Sure'n hell not the rag heads. What about the Japs?"

"Slant-eyed sons of bitches are clever enough. But why?" He scanned the sea around them. "Maybe they're somehow watching and enjoying this right now." They were taunting him.

This went beyond just pulling the wings off flies or placing a scorpion on a hot plate. The loss of the Nature's Child would be a blow to the company's pride and prestige. It was a financial loss easily borne by men in their trade. However, it would be resented more as an inconvenience than as a serious threat.

A loss of personnel would be more serious, since that went even deeper to the ego and pride of the organization. One could tolerate material losses as a hazard of doing business, but one would not tolerate the loss of family, friends, or employees. With this attitude, Trope ordered the captain to take whatever steps were necessary to save the personnel on board, even if it meant sacrificing the ship.

"I'm going to buy a bigger, better ship. I'll call her Nature's Child II. And by God I'll shove a hot poker up the ass of the scumbag responsible for this."

"Jeez, Hermine. Calm down. You'll have a stroke. We'll get the jerks that did this. The boys'll fix 'em."

"Yeah, Yeah. I know. It's the loss of face. They'll be laughing at me. Me, the boss of the coast."

"No. No they won't. They wouldn't dare. They know you're the man," Adams reassured him.

"You're right. The hell with the boat. Just make sure the captain and crew are safe. Let's get out of here."

The captain was relieved that he wasn't expected to go down with the ship. It wouldn't have been optional if Trope called it that way.

"Abandon ship. Man the life rafts." There were four Danish rafts, two port and two starboard. Each raft was rated for six men. All carried food, water and emergency supplies.

Adams had moved off about 100 meters from the Nature's Child to evaluate the situation. The captain and the primary security crew debated fighting the fire and for a time gave it a try.

"Forget it. She's lost. I'll not have you dying for nothing. Abandon ship," Trope screamed.

They joined their mates in the rafts. As the crew settled into the life rafts they saw their leaders easing slowly away in the Whaler.

"Where the hell are they going?"

"To get help stupid. Now lend a hand." The Captain watched Trope move away with a mixture of gratitude and hope.

CHAPTER TWENTY THREE
KARMA

"I'm telling you, Hermine, we should keep the boat near the rafts because the security personnel have weapons with them. Whoever was responsible for this might show up." He had a point. "We'd have better defensive fire by having five vessels.

We might even be able to set up a cross-fire if someone tried to attack."

"You know, you have some good points there, Terrance." For a change, he thought. "The clustered firepower and multiplicity of targets would be better defensively. But . . . I believe anyone coming after us would home in on the rafts, all lit by the strobe lights. Or they might home in on the EPIRB signals. The rafts would be vulnerable to small arms fire." His lips curled and his mouth twisted into a sinister sneer.

"Decoys, the rafts would be excellent decoys. They would attract the attention of an attacker. We escaped on this boat by sheer chance. The enemy wouldn't be expecting us to have it. Also, we can make much better speed by abandoning the rafts and striking out toward shore. Meanwhile, if a firefight erupted, it would further delay the enemy. The confusion created would benefit us."

"Jim, which way is land?"

"My best guess is that way." He pointed off to their port

quarter.

"Lacking a compass or anything to tell us otherwise, let's go that way," Hermine suggested.

They had fuel, food and water and plenty of weapons and ammunition. All were in good health with no injuries. The boat was well built. They even had lovely companions to make the voyage less disagreeable. He felt comfortable and self- confident.

"Branngg . . . Whomph." The Whaler had been under power for less than 25 minutes when loud explosions ripped the water beneath the transom. The boat coasted to a stop.

"Jim, check the stern," Adams commanded. He scanned the horizon, searching for any threat.

"I'll watch, you help Jim," Trope ordered.

With the help of the mate, he tilted up the outboards.

"I'll be dipped in shit." The bottom parts of both outboards had been blown away. "How did they do that?

"Beats me, but they ruptured the transom while they were at it." Rushing water drenched their feet.

It was not catastrophic damage, just bad enough to cause a troublesome leak, as seawater started to invade the cockpit of the boat. If all six people bailed, they could keep up with the water inflow and prevent water from filling the cockpit. In any event the boat would not sink, but it would be impossible for them to continue this vigorous bailing for a protracted time period. Eventually they would have to put up with being wet if not with the danger of sinking. The girls tired first and water started to edge up into the cockpit.

Soon the men also fatigued. The water was rapidly rising. The boat was in no danger of sinking. Whalers have been cut in half and still both ends floated independently. It was more a matter of discomfort that first troubled Trope, Adams and the rest of the group huddled with them.

"Terry, I don't like this." Trope realized they no longer had a means of reaching shore unaided, and there was no sign of the ship or the other rafts.

"Looks like we're on our own," Jim commented dryly.

There was a two-man raft tucked up in the bow of the Whaler, but Trope didn't even want to think about having to use that. He tended to be a trifle claustrophobic and a two-man raft wasn't exactly spacious.

"Gas. I smell gasoline," Hermine shrieked. "Look!" A slick was spreading from the tanks.

The raft started to look inviting. Trope didn't know when the gas would catch fire, but based on the events that led to this juncture, he sensed it would.

"Give me a hand," Jim ordered the girl. They dragged a fiberglass container from the front deck to the transom. Jim yanked vigorously on a long rope attached to the canister.

"Kapow!" The top popped off. "Pppwhisssh . . ." Another Danish six-man raft started to inflate.

Adams and Trope looked at each other and at the mate. They could have hugged him.

Jim smiled. "I may be old, but I ain't retarded, and I didn't get old by being careless."

Trope mentally wrote the man a big bonus check. When they got to shore he would show his appreciation in a tangible way. Without being told to do so, Adams jumped into the water and climbed the boarding ladder to pull himself into the life raft. He checked for booby traps or anything that would threaten their safety. "Clear," he yelled.

Evie and her friend got into the life raft with Trope and Adams. The mate and his girl were still standing on the boat.

"I'll try to stop the leak and see if I can fix the transom," Jim yelled to Hermine. "I'll check the cabin for the other raft and supplies," the girl volunteered.

Trope and Adams started to paddle away from the disabled boat. Gradually, the life raft drifted away from the Boston Whaler. Ultimately they lost track of the boat. Adams looked for signs of a boat fire or explosion, but could discern nothing. When dawn broke they found themselves completely isolated. There was no sign of the Nature's Child, the four other life rafts or the Boston Whaler. By mid-day they had seen one or two small boats in the vicinity and they'd fired flares and let off smoke signals, but failed to attract attention. Later in the afternoon they saw a high-speed cigarette boat cutting across the horizon, then turning gradually toward them.

"It's a miracle," declared Evie. The boat seemed to be headed toward a point only three or four hundred meters west of their position.

"Look," she yelled. "It's coming toward us."

Gradually the boat veered until it was pointed at them almost directly.

"Light off some smoke," Hermine shouted to Adams.

He lit off another smoke signal, Hermine fired a flare and Evie started blowing the whistle from the emergency kit. Trope turned on the strobe light.

"We're okay, they see us." The boat got closer.

"*Bloommm . . . Bloommm . . .*" They heard the engines throttle back. Smoke billowed and the engines backfired as the boat dropped her bow and slowed.

Adams was still apprehensive. Cautiously he pulled a GLOCK 19 pistol from his jacket and worked the action to load the chamber. He pulled a small pair of Tasco binoculars from his other pocket and searched the cigarette boat.

"The Foxy Lady" was printed on her bow. One look at the operator clarified the name of the vessel. She was awesome, very dark-skinned, probably African or Haitian.

"Damn," Adams leered. "Look at that." Her hair was raven black and flowed over her shoulders. Only a string bikini and sunglasses prevented nudity.

"Whoa, Nellie." His glasses rested upon her companion, a tall red-haired girl. "Big Red, you're mine," he thought.

"No threat," he said, pocketing his pistol. Adams felt paranoid, but that was his job.

"Need any help?" Big Red called as The Foxy Lady glided to the raft.

"That," Trope said to himself, "has to be the stupidest question I ever heard. What the hell did she think, finding a life raft alone in the middle of the freaking ocean?" He stifled a bitter response and said, "Yes. Myself and my companions would appreciate a ride to shore."

Red went to the stern of the boat, threw the boarding ladder over the side, then tossed a line to Adams and gently towed the life raft to the rear of the speedboat.

"Why don't you two girls come on board first? You fellows could assist them out of the raft." Red extended her hand.

"Okay." First one girl and then the other came on board the speedboat.

"What the . . .?" Adams was full of self-congratulations as he prepared to board the cigarette. His glee was short-lived.

Clikk . . . crunk. Adams looked up to see the barrel of an AK 47 aimed at his face. It was cocked and Red wasn't smiling.

Clack . . . clunck. He heard another familiar sound. The black girl was aiming an Uzi carbine at Trope.

"Into the water right now, gentlemen."

They hesitated.

Thup, thup, thup . . . A burst howled from the AK, perforating the life raft.

"Into the water please," the Foxy Lady repeated.

"If you insist." Trope jumped. Big choice, go down with the raft or go swimming. The water didn't look so bad after all.

Big Red looked at the two girls. "Ladies, you have two choices, accompany us and keep your mouths shut, or join your friends in the water. It's up to you."

The decision was unanimous. Both girls felt they would prefer to remain on board. With that, the dark girl walked over to the rail.

"I don't want you to think I'm harsh," Foxy Lady declared, "and I certainly wouldn't want to strand you here without any help." She threw the men two life jackets. "I suggest you wear these."

The jackets were class threes, just barely providing enough floatation to keep the head above water in a mild swell.

"I don't wish to sound ungrateful, but are you planning on leaving us stranded?" Trope tried to distract the girls.

Neither Trope nor Adams was experienced in survival but they both knew that if the water got rough the Class Threes would be useless.

"All right, bitches, just watch him while I get out my pistol." Adams wondered if he could drop both girls before one of them could nail him. He would be firing up hill facing into the sun.

"Screw this." His targets made difficult shots. Sea swells were moving him and the Foxy Lady. Also the girls were not remaining stationary. Very smart, he thought.

"Will you fire or won't you?" He fingered the pistol. How badly soaked was the ammunition? It would be blind luck to hit either girl. If they were half as handy as they appeared to be, the other would surely cut him to pieces. "Not this time, Ladies." He elected not to try the pistol.

Anyway, he assured himself, as soon as they got back to port, his girls would notify the authorities and help would quickly be on the way. The water wasn't too cold; the seas were relatively calm. His chances were still better than shooting it out at point blank range.

"Now I really don't want you folks to think unkindly of us," Foxy Lady drawled as Red stooped down and brought out two Locators.

"We are not inhospitable." Red threw the radar reflectors over the transom in the general direction of the struggling swimmers. "Naturally we wouldn't leave you without a way of being found."

The black girl addressed the men desperately treading water. "Y'all kin use those Locators. I understand you people are responsible for the manufacture of these high quality products."

Trope looked at Adams. Adams looked at Trope.

"Shit." Trope swore under his breath.

"No, no, really. We sold that off to a big company a long time ago. It's not us," Adams pleaded.

"No matter. I certainly hope they do a good job in bringing rescue to you." She looked piercingly at Terry. "You may wish to think of two Haitian men who used to work for you."

Adams wanted to throw up.

"Your Jamaican friend was most unkind to them. While

you are waiting for someone to be kind to you, possibly you will wish to think upon such matters, my friend."

Trope wondered how these girls knew he had been connected to the Locator. Was this little accident staged by Mark Hansen, or was it the work of his own associates? Had his own people decided to trash him for some reason? It didn't make sense. And Mark just wasn't that bright or that brave. The Washington deal proved that.

The black girl must know about the accident with Linda and the subsequent clean-up. Maybe his own people had set him up.

"Hey, I'm really sorry about your brothers. We didn't even know they had family." As if that made it all right.

"Why sink the boat? You're killing innocent men . . . The crew never hurt you." He was talking for his life.

"Hey Mon, save your energy. You just may be a'needing it." The lovely Haitian slowly advanced the throttles, easing the Foxy Lady up to speed. She never looked back.

Trope and Adams drifted for about an hour. Finally Trope, swearing again muttered, "I don't give a damn, there's only one way to tell . . . try one of those things." They knew the Locators might be booby-trapped or they might not work after all.

"What difference does it make if it's a grenade? At least it'll be over quick," sneered Adams. Daylight was fading and the water was growing colder, the waves higher.

"Screw it. I'll try mine," Adams volunteered.

He tore the seal from his unit and removed the top. As he pulled the red inflation handle, teeth clenched, he fearfully waited for an explosion.

"Psssss . . ." He heard the expected hissing sound as helium gas flowed from the cartridge, but there was no inflation of the balloon.

"Oh . . . God . . ." Looking down, he realized that the gas was forcing liquid from the device. Marker dye, he thought. Wrong color. He lifted the Locator. Red liquid ran out onto him as it spurted away from the base of the unit.

"Blood. You dirty bitches. It's blood." Horrified, he realized that the liquid was flowing into the water all around him. Desperately he struggled in vain to stem the flow.

Adams threw the unit as far away as he could. Blood flowed as the Locator drifted under the waves.

Trope watched; he saw what had happened. He tried to swim away from Adams immediately after throwing away his own Locator.

He wondered if it contained a bomb, blood or a balloon. He wouldn't take the chance to find out.

Adams swam away from Trope. He figured that the blood would drift with the current. He guessed the current was headed northwest, so he tried to head southeast, but found it difficult to make progress against the current.

Trope, aided by the current, was distancing himself from Adams, who was remaining relatively stationary. The blood stretched out in the water, heading from Adams and pointing toward Trope. Adams wasn't much of a seaman, but he knew in these waters at this time of the year it wouldn't be long before he was visited by those large-toothed grinning men in gray suits.

"Should I just swim for the bottom and breathe in deeply?" he deliberated. "They say drowning is not such a painful way to die. Maybe I should get it over with."

"Hell no. I've got my pistol. It'll stop anything . . . and with 19 shots I could kill any big fish that comes near." Adams was certain he had a chance. By his reckoning it was less than forty-five minutes before he saw the first triangular fins cutting the water. Some time passed before the first shark nosed Adams, and still longer before a fish of any magnitude arrived.

Occasionally Trope could see his brother-in-law when phases of the waves were right and both men were on the crests at the same time. Trope could make out the fins surrounding Adams. It was like watching a surrealistic dance.

He saw a flash. "Brannggg . . ." The report from the pistol shot drifted over the waves. Adams was trying to defend himself.

"Merciful Jesus. He has more guts than I gave him credit for," thought Trope. "Branngg . . ." Another report followed in quick succession by three more . . . But instead of more gunfire, the next sound was a pathetic groan drifting across the waves.

"Why didn't you yell?" Somehow it wasn't what he expected. In the movies it was always a piercing shriek or a loud call for help. This sad, pitiful cry was worse, far worse. So brief, so quickly stilled.

Cresting on a wave, he saw the water swirling with fins but saw nothing of Adams and heard no more.

"Probably just as well. Who needs a slow motion preview of his own?" He fought for control. Even so, Trope realized his time must be short.

Despite the furious swirl that was developing southeast from him, Trope saw a few triangular fins spaced out between him and the riling water. It was impossible to tell their direction in the fading light, but he didn't need to see to know. He realized he was downstream of the path of the blood and carnage. It wouldn't be long before he too was visited.

Hermine felt an unrestrained rush of fear and relief, relief that the sharks had not eaten him yet. "What kind of person are you? Have you no shame?" His mother's words stabbed at him.

Your own brother-in-law, you bastard, he thought. As long as it is not you — Right? You son-of-a-bitch.

He had heard of gut-wrenching fear but never understood what it meant. Now as his own guts were twisted in terror and he felt his bowels empty involuntarily into his trousers, at last he understood.

"Fuck . . . even this . . ."

His life didn't flash before his eyes in those last minutes. Maybe it was too ugly to bear repeating. Maybe he was too terrified. Maybe he had to prove to himself he could die at least as bravely as Terry.

"Mom. Oh my God." As more fins appeared he knew his time was used up. He held the crucifix in his right hand. His mother had given it to him. She had died despairing the life he had chosen. Was she now to gain solace that in his last moments it was to that crucifix he would cling?

"Hail Mary full of grace . . ." It was to the same God and

Blessed Virgin that his mother had introduced him, that he screamed his last pleas for help as a large hammerhead severed his right shoulder, crushing his rib cage, causing a rib to puncture his heart.

It was a mercifully quick death for a man who had ruled over the slow humiliating despair of so many others.

Mark would have been bitterly disappointed that his enemy had died so quickly . . . with a plea for grace upon his lips. Had there been a philosopher among the sharks, he might have wondered if this man was forgiven for all his sins by virtue of his necessarily brief simple pleas in the last moments of his troubled life.

Neither Mark nor any philosophers were present as the hammerheads quarreled for the choice morsels of Trope's body while the sun bobbed over the horizon.

CHAPTER TWENTY FOUR
AFTERMATH

"Oh Melodie, you are so fine!" The speedboat driver congratulated herself. "That's two white boys never gonna mess about my family again." Nothing she could do would bring back her brothers—but this helped.

"None of my business, but what are you going to do with the money?" Red asked.

"Get legal, get my green card," she laughed. "Then bring my momma over from Haiti." She looked back at her new friend. "What about you?"

"Pay some bills . . . get started again . . ." She tossed her head, shaking her long hair. "You'd have done it free and so would I." Her eyes narrowed like a pit viper's. "I wish we could've watched."

"They had more chance than my brothers." She turned the boat into an inlet. "But I didn't want to watch." Evil comes back three times, she'd been told.

"There's much worse things than dying," Red hissed. "I really wanted to see it all."

Melodie had seen people made ill by much less hate than that. "That's the most you've spoke in three weeks, girl."

"Big mouths get people dead." Unexpectedly her eyes lost their rage. She almost smiled. "I've got a bunch of living to do yet."

"Tell the truth," she agreed.

Melodie wondered if the "trainer" would be at the dock to check on them. He was interested in their safety and survival, not just in their getting the "task" —as he called it — completed. Both girls sensed a genuine interest on his behalf, and it had made the training easier; particularly when they had problems learning the weapons, which tended to frighten the Haitian girl. Before dumping the boat she had one more job to do.

Melodie guided the boat to an open area near a sandy beach. "All right ladies, come on up. You're going over the side." They were approaching a swimming beach north of Stuart.

"Evie, you and your friend are alive by our generosity. We don't believe you were deeply involved with those people," the tall red-headed girl cautioned. "If you want to stay pretty and not wind up in the Harem of a Libyan sheik, you'll keep your mouths shut. You never were on the ship and you know nothing. Right?"

No mouse ever viewed a cobra with greater terror than Evie viewed her benefactor. "We don't know anything and we don't want to know anything. All right?" The two girls cowered together.

"Can you swim?"

They nodded.

"Here's a water-tight change purse with fifty dollars for each of you. Also in the purse you'll find a bunch of quarters. There's a phone right up there by the highway. You'll have no trouble getting a cab." She looked at the girls. "It's a short swim. Be careful and remember what I said. You'll be watched. "

Melodie let out a sigh of relief as she docked the Foxy Lady in a small marina just north of Palm Beach. She and Red walked over to their waiting cars and left. Shortly thereafter, a man walked up, jumped in the boat, cast off and headed up the Intercoastal Waterway.

He was slight of build and wiry. Clearly at home at the

helm, he fired up the engines and made deliberate progress south at 25 knots, periodically slowing down for manatee zones or to avoid disturbing any of the yachts resting at anchor on the Intercoastal Waterway. He reached a less traveled section of the waterway, pulled near shore, then dropped anchor. Next he dropped a two-man inflatable raft over the side. Nothing he had done had attracted any attention up to that point. After wiping the fittings, wheel, throttle quadrant and bright work, he left the boat by paddling the raft to shore, then walked through the undergrowth to a car he had parked there earlier.

"That's one small swim for man." He laughed heartily, threw the deflated raft into the trunk and headed north toward Orlando.

"Remember the toy you loaned me." He spoke into the cellular phone. "I'm sorry, but I lost it."

"That's okay, it was used anyway," came the reply. "Have a nice vacation and say 'hi' to everyone for me."

"Will do." He accelerated up the Florida State Turnpike. "You take care of yourself now. Don't go getting a cold."

"Thanks. See ya."

Sean was relieved. The message meant all had gone well. He was free to have the police called with a missing boat report. "Yes, Sergeant, the cigarette boat next to my dock is missing. The owner is out of the country and we're trying to reach her." He nodded. "Namibia I believe." He chuckled.

"No sir, didn't see or hear a thing. Probably just some kids out joy riding." He could hardly restrain himself. "You're welcome. Have a nice day."

The following day in the newspaper, there was a brief article: "SIX MISSING, FEARED LOST. The luxury yacht Nature's Child experienced some type of motor difficulties and evidently caught fire. Her crew of twelve escaped in lifeboats and no one was seriously injured. The boat went to the bottom after being abandoned. Six people remain missing: two unidentified women, thought to be models; two employees of the holding company who owned the boat; the first mate, and his girlfriend. The Coast Guard suspended search at sunset and plans to resume tomorrow."

In a separate article appearing several days later, it was noted that a Russian trawler had found two more survivors of the yacht. The first mate and his girlfriend were safe, leaving four people missing and presumed drowned. The mate and his friend had been transferred to an American vessel. As yet there were no details on the missing people.

By this time Walt had driven through North Florida and was in Atlanta. He turned in the rental car and subsequently boarded an airplane to go to Los Angeles where he stayed for three days. From there he took a 747 to Honolulu and after a layover he went to Auckland to go sailing with a friend anxiously awaiting him.

He took with him newspaper articles from the Los Angeles paper that might be of interest to his friend. Another person also read with interest the articles in the Fort Lauderdale newspapers.

"LADY AND THE SHARK. LOCAL GIRL MAKES GOOD. Daphne Leyland, recent University of Miami graduate, has rocked the industry with the introduction of a hit toy line. Seen pictured below, Miss Leyland is displaying the 'Pool Shark' one of three new toy items introduced by her firm at the Toy Fair in Atlanta."

Daphne studied the articles with great intensity. "Damn." She frowned as she read the part about the loss of the vessel. "I wish that hadn't been necessary." She had misgivings about her part in it. She hadn't been raised to hurt anyone or anything and had great respect for all of God's creations. She was relieved to learn that the entire crew was safely recovered. There was a certain pride in craftsmanship; she knew if anyone else had designed, developed or implemented any of the programs or devices employed in the "task" that there could have been unintentional loss of life. This had been the challenge. Injury to innocent people, if any were on the boat, would have been a cross for her to bear.

Even if people were evil, Daphne felt she had no right to harm them. She had accepted the "task" knowing that she might suffer even more severe penalties than just her own personal guilt feelings if anything major went wrong and they were apprehended by the police; or worse yet, by the mob. It was a calculated risk, which she had weighed heavily before making her choice.

Yet layered over these thoughts was the image of Linda's body after its recovery from the canal.

Just as in a military operation, information had been limited to a need to know. This was added insurance in the event that a part of the operation came unraveled. Therefore, much of what transpired would remain unknown to Daphne. Still, somehow she knew that fate, or karma, or God in his infinite wisdom, had allowed them to strike down the people who had taken her friend's life. Again she read the article in the newspaper. The success of the new company in some way equated in her mind to a sort of infinite approval of her actions.

Mark suffered no mixed feelings. He laughed aloud as he read and reread the newspapers. Content, he slowly shredded the papers, then gently scattered them in the wake of his sailboat. He watched the seawater fold over the scraps, saturating them. Joining the sea they drifted down, sinking into the depths until they were gone. Gone. It began in the sea. It was fitting that it ended there. Mark sheeted in the sails, adjusted his course. His thoughts moved from Bimini, from Linda, from the Locator, through his present financial success and into the future. As he scanned the horizon he was propelled toward that future. A future with Walt and Abe, and . . . Daphne? He wondered. He drove the boat hard toward Auckland.

9 781893 302082